DRUGS
of the
DREAMING

"Gianluca Toro and Benjamin Thomas have made an invaluable contribution to the literature on psychoactive substances by tackling the vast but hitherto neglected domain of the use of oneirogenic plants and drugs throughout history, around the world. Using a multidisciplinary approach that draws from ethnobotany, anthropology, medical research, chemistry, and the recorded experiences of "psychonauts" who have experimented with many of these compounds, they have compiled a rigorously researched, fascinating, exhaustive survey of the planet's oneirogens, ranging all the way from recently popularized herbs such as *Salvia divinorum* and *Calea zacatechichi* to ancient Egyptian, Greek, Celtic, Amazonian, African and medieval potions; to vitamins and hormones; to dream-inducing cheeses and fish species!

"The extensive lists of the world's known oneirogens and the generous bibliography are treasure troves in and of themselves. As the authors make clear, there is much we don't know about many of these tantalizing substances and the states they induce. In fact, this is really a nascent field, but this book marks a giant step forward in an exciting new front in the exploration of humanity's never-ending thirst for heightened states of consciousness. No one with a serious interest in the rich lore of psychotropic substances should be without this book."

J. P. HARPIGNIES, EDITOR OF
VISIONARY PLANT CONSCIOUSNESS

DRUGS
of the
DREAMING

Oneirogens:
Salvia divinorum and
Other Dream-Enhancing Plants

Gianluca Toro and Benjamin Thomas

Park Street Press
Rochester, Vermont

Park Street Press
One Park Street
Rochester, Vermont 05767
www.ParkStPress.com

Park Street Press is a division of Inner Traditions International

Library of Congress Cataloging-in-Publication Data

Toro, Gianluca, 1969–
  Drugs of the dreaming : oneirogens : Salvia divinorum and other dream-enhancing plants / Gianluca Toro and Benjamin Thomas.
      p. ; cm.
  Includes bibliographical references and index.
  ISBN-13: 978-1-59477-174-3 (pbk.)
  ISBN-10: 1-59477-174-X (pbk.)
  1. Hallucinogenic drugs. 2. Hallucinogenic plants. 3. Salvia divinorum. 4. Dreams. 5. Altered states of consciousness. 6. Ethnopharmacology. I. Thomas, Benjamin, 1970– II. Title.
  [DNLM: 1. Plants, Medicinal—physiology. 2. Dreams—drug effects. 3. Ethnopharmacology. 4. Hallucinogens—pharmacology. QV 766 T686d 2007]
  RM324.8T67 2007
  615'.7883—dc22

                                                                          2007004054

Printed and bound in the United States by Lake Book Manufacturing

10   9   8   7   6   5   4   3   2   1

Text design and layout by Virginia Scott Bowman
This book was typeset in Sabon and Avenir with Arepo and Avenir as the display typefaces

Contents

Ayahuasca • *Brugmansia* spp. • *Calea zacatechichi*
Casimiroa edulis • *Clematis virginiana*
Cymbopogon densiflorus • *Cypripedium calceolus*
Desfontainia spinosa • *Duboisi hopwoodii*
Elaeagnus sp. • *Entada rheedii* • *Erythrina americana*
Galbulimima belgraveana • *Heimia salicifolia*
Homalomena sp. • *Hyoscyamus muticus*
Kaempferia galanga • *Lycopodium* spp.
Mimosa hostilis • *Myristica fragrans* • *Salvia divinorum*
Scirpus sp. • *Silene capensis* • *Turbina corymbosa*
Ugni candollei • *Xeromphis* sp.

Foreword

One of the most recondite and least investigated areas of ethnomedicine involves the oneirogens, or dream-inducing plants, of which the scientific prototype might be *Calea zacatechichi,* known as *thle-pelakano.* It is used by the Chontal Indians of Mexico, who drink infusions of the dried leaves and likewise smoke them in cigarettes. This has generally been regarded as a special category of psychoptic, or visionary, plants.

Evidently phytochemical investigation of such oneirogenic plants is hampered by the fact that dreams occur naturally, spontaneously, and unpredictably, rendering difficult the development of suitable psychonautic bioassays to guide fractionation. On the other hand, the reality of this category of ethnomedicines is undeniable, and it has been documented among diverse cultures on several continents. Moreover, preliminary investigation of *Calea zacatechichi* (which, however, failed to isolate any oneirogenic active principle[s]) lent support to the notion that it favors or enhances dreaming. In fact, there has been a substantial market in this so-called Dream Herb and its Dream Drops extract (this being a trademark of the first company to market it—the Jungle/Botanical Preservation Corps), mostly via mail order from a large number of shamanic plant dealers. Modern interest in so-called lucid dreaming has no doubt stimulated renewed interest in this and other oneirogenic plants.

Happily some of this obscurity has now been dispelled by the publication of *Drugs of the Dreaming* by Gianluca Toro and Benjamin

Thomas. This comprehensive book explores dreaming and the concept of oneirogenesis, then details a large number of documented oneirogenic plants used by many indigenous cultures. The scope is ethnobiological as opposed to strictly ethnobotanical, inasmuch as a handful of oneirogenic animals are also examined, not to mention pure chemical compounds, both natural and artificial, as well as foodstuffs. Ethnopharmacognosy has long been in debt to Benjamin Thomas for focusing his research on fascinating and little-studied Papua New Guinea. This book continues that research, with important new documentation of the dream-man complex there, involving several poorly documented, putative psychoactive plants.

This is an original and pioneering book, which hopefully will lead to "sweet dreams" for the oneirically inclined.

Jonathan Ott
Rancho Xochiatl
February 25, 2006

Jonathan Ott is an American chemist and founder of the Natural Products Company, a chemical manufacturing firm producing natural product neurotoxins for use in biomedical research. Ott is the author of many books, including *Hallucinogenic Plants of North America* (1976), *The Cacahuatl Eater: Ruminations of an Unabashed Chocolate Eater* (1985), *Pharmacotheon: Entheogenic Drugs, Their Plant Sources and History* (1993), *The Age of Entheogens & The Angel's Dictionary* (1995), and *Pharmacophilia: or The Natural Paradises* (1997) and numerous articles on psychoactive plants published in journals including *Journal of Psychedelic Drugs, Journal of Psychoactive Drugs,* and *Eleusis: Journal of Psychoactive Plants & Compounds.*

Acknowledgments

I wish to thank D. Mas De Xaxars from La Garriga (Barcelona) for the information provided and the encouragement, and Jonathan Ott for his kind foreword.

— G. Toro

For Danielle Wiseman.
I am indebted to Jonathan Ott, Giorgio Samorini, Albert Hofmann, and Alexander T. Shulgin for their support of this work.

— B. Thomas

1

Non-Ordinary States of Consciousness

Humanity has historically shown an acute interest in modifying the ordinary state of consciousness in order to achieve "other" states, denoted as "non-ordinary" or "altered," in which the emotional and sensory perceptions occur in ways distinct from the usual ones. It is a phenomenon that could be considered innate to the species, a universal behavioral constant without distinction of evolutionary period, culture, or race, which has followed, follows, and always will follow us.

This tendency is demonstrated all over the world by past artistic and literary evidence, by the present customs of many tribal populations, and in modern cultures. The means for achieving such altered states is part of our heritage. It has been handed down to us as knowledge conveying the properties and uses of psychoactive plants. Reaching far back in time to prehistoric rock art, we find the depiction of psychoactive mushrooms or plants and images that can be interpreted as representing an altered state of consciousness. In our own age we can point to the use of natural psychotropic preparations in the Amazonian rain forest (ayahuasca) or among African tribes (iboga root in Gabon), as well as to the consumption of synthetic drugs in modern Western cultures (ecstasy above all). Such a tendency is considered biologically normal, not exclusive of the human species but also typical of other animals.

The alteration of the ordinary state of consciousness can be obtained by means of many techniques discovered and perfected by

1

humans: including sensory and sleep deprivation, physical mortification, fasting, dance, music, meditation, and the employment of psychoactive drugs originating in plants and animals. The consumption of psychoactive plants may be the most ancient and widespread of all consciousness-altering techniques; its origin dates back to the Stone Age.

But why does human nature continually seek the alteration of consciousness? Our motivations are numerous and complex. Surely the more immediate, natural, and instinctive one is the search for pleasure. Such a motivation is at the base of various other human behaviors. But just as important may be the search for a deeper comprehension and interpretation of our surroundings and of life itself as well as the search for an adaptation strategy to cope with changes in our reality.

The dream state is a non-ordinary state of consciousness that we commonly and spontaneously experience every night, the prototype of the hallucinatory experience. In this sense, inducing dreams and developing the oneiric imagination is a way to experience an altered state of consciousness.

Since ancient times dreams have been important in the life of many traditional populations and the basis not only of spiritual and religious development but also of intellectual development, permitting a direct contact with the realm of the supernatural. Dream-inducing plants are considered sacred; they are the source of divinity manifesting in the human body and acting on the mind.

Psychoactive Drug Classification

The use of drugs is very ancient, but the reflection on their specific effects is relatively recent and dates back to the beginning of the eighteenth century. For example, in the *Encyclopédie* (1747–1766) of D. Diderot and J. B. D'Alembert, under the item *Drogue*, the only specifically mentioned drug is opium, listed as having therapeutic properties and inebriant effects producing a surprising cheerfulness in the heart and stunning the mind with charming ideas and pleasures.

In 1858 Italian psychopharmacologist P. Mantegazza, in "Sulle virtù

igieniche e medicinali della coca e sugli alimenti nervosi in generale"
[On the Hygienic and Medicinal Properties of Coca and on Nervine
Nourishments in General], classifies the psychoactive substances (named
"nervous nourishments") into three families: alcoholic, alkaloidal, and
aromatic. The first family comprises two tribes: fermented (wine, beer,
cider, hydromel, chicha) and distilled (brandy, rum, gin, rosolii, anis-
ette, arrak, different liqueurs). The tribes of the second family are caffeic
(coffee, tea, mate, guaranà, gorù nuts, *Celastrum edulis*) and narcotic
(opium, hashish, kawa, betel, amanita, coca, ayahuasca, tobacco), while
in the third family we find various spices.

The first modern classification of drugs, which is still used today,
was proposed in 1924 by pharmacologist Louis Lewin. In *Phantastica*
he writes about the agents capable of effecting a modification of the
cerebral functions, which are used to obtain agreeable sensations of
excitement or peace of mind. The classes proposed are Euphorica (mental sedatives: opium and its components and derivatives, and cocaine),
Phantastica (hallucinogens or "drugs of illusion": peyote, hemp, and
some solanaceous plants), Inebriantia (cerebral excitants: alcohol, chlo-
roform, ether, benzine), Hypnotica (sleep-inducers: chloral, veronal, sul-
phonal), and Excitantia (mental stimulants: coffee, tobacco, betel).

In 1961 Jean Delay and Pierre Deniker proposed a pharmaco-
clinic classification of the psychotropic substances based on that of
Lewin. There are three groups: psycholeptics, reducing the cerebral
tonus (hypnotics, tranquillants, sedatives, neuroleptics, mood regula-
tors); psychoanaleptics or psychotonics, increasing the cerebral tonus
(antidepressants, excitants, vigilance stimulants); and psychodysleptics
perturbing the cerebral tonus (alcohol and derivatives, stupefying substances, hallucinogens).

We note that in past drug classifications there wasn't a specific class
for substances capable of inducing dreams (oneirogens), though it might
be assumed that they were included among the hallucinogens. The intro-
duction of this class of drugs in the 1970s is relatively recent, and it is the
consequence of the recognition of a peculiar effect, in some way distinct
from that of other drugs.

In 2004 Dr. Lucien Giacomoni revised the classification of psychoactive drugs pertaining to the psychodysleptic (PDL) class on the basis of associated syndromes. In particular, he identifies a subclass of substances responsible for a syndrome similar to that caused by the hallucinogens *sensu stricto*—the hypnagogens or narco-psychodysleptics corresponding to the classical oneirogens.

Hypnagogens cause and accentuate the images rising while falling asleep, that time between dream and reality. They are equally narcotic and/or PDL according to their action. In this subclass Giacomoni puts *Calea zacatechichi, Galbulimima belgraveana, Heimia salicifolia, Scirpus atrovirens, Silene capensis, Souroubea crassipetala, S. guianensis,* and the mushrooms *Lycoperdon marginatum* and *L. mixtecorum.*

Giacomoni also identifies another subclass among the substances provoking a syndrome similar to the hallucinogenic one. This is represented by the pseudo-hallucinogens and comprises all the plants rich in essential oils, among which the best-known example is *Artemisia absinthium* (wormwood). Here we find two plants with supposed oneirogenic activity, *Cymbopogon densiflorus* and *Kaempferia galanga.*

Dale Pendell, in his classification of drugs, identifies a particular class named Rhapsodica, where we find, besides *A. absinthium,* the classical oneirogen *C. zacatechichi.*

Moreover, Claude Rifat[1] proposes a distinction between "pre-oneirogen" (or "hypnagogic") and "true oneirogen." Pre-oneirogens cause an increase in the production of hypnagogic imagery (perceived in the transition between waking and sleep) as well as hypnopompic imagery (perceived in the transition between sleep and waking). Examples of pre-oneirogens are psilocin (one of the active principles of some mushroom species, above all in the genus *Psilocybe*) and Δ^9-Tetrahydrocannabinol (Δ^9-THC), the active principle of *Cannabis sativa.* The term *hallucinogen* is considered a synonym of *pre-oneirogen* and is intended as an inducer of a perception without an external source.

The presence of effects typical of each class of psychoactive substances allows one to classify such substances in a specific class. Such classification is first of all physiopathological and secondly chemical (according to the chemical nature of the active principles involved), rather than botanical or mycological. This means that the same pharmacological action can be associated with compounds of very different chemical structures.

Oneirogen Characteristics

According to Jonathan Ott, an oneirogen is a drug that stimulates dreams or hypnagogic phenomena in superficial stages of sleep, where hypnagogic refers to drowsiness, or preceding sleep, or early, light stage of sleep.[2] This neologism is based on the word *oneiromantic* first used by French poet Charles Baudelaire in *Les Paradis Artificiels (The Artificial Paradises)*.

Oneirogen derives from Greek, literally meaning "that which produces dream." The neologism "oneirogenic" was first used by José Luis Díaz to describe the effects of the plant *C. zacatechichi* that is used in Mexico to induce dream visions. It has been suggested that *C. zacatechichi* is the prototype of the oneirogens, or dream-inducing drugs.

Specifically, oneirogens produce the main subjective effects observed in ordinary or conscious dream; the prototypes are salvinorin A (active principle of *Salvia divinorum*), which at low doses is considered a pre-oneirogen, ibogaine (active principle of *Tabernanthe iboga*) and ketamine (a dissociative anaesthetic).[3] According to Robert Goutarel, such action manifests itself in the disconnection of the "I" from the exoreality (the external world) and the reconnection in the endoreality (the inner world).

Generally, the hallucinogenic activity is considered distinct from the oneirogenic one, because a hallucinogen has an influence on the vigilant conscience, while an oneirogen has little effect on it, acting instead specifically on the oneiric production during sleep. Moreover, the hallucination has the property of "being outside the observer," while the dream corresponds to an inner content, because it is the result of the elaboration of information proceeding from the brain.

In fact, such a distinction doesn't seem to be clear. By the beginning of the 1800s, a close correlation between the content of hallucination and that of dream was evident. The dream is considered the prototype of the hallucinatory experience; this means that dream and hallucination are phenomena similar in nature, primarily in relation to the activity of the cerebral areas involved. Moreover, a hallucinogen can manifest its action not only in the waking state but also in dream.

One also has to consider that it is possible to characterize the prototypical effect of oneirogenic substances as inducing a state of repose, rest, or sleep, and feelings of peace, tranquillity, or calmness. However, the substances that correspond to such a broad definition are great in number, and it would be difficult to define their real oneirogenic activity.

Oneirogens can logically be divided into two categories, those distinguished as true oneirogens (acting directly on the process of dream production) and pre-oneirogens (involved in the production of hypnagogic imagery). In the present text, this second category will be excluded because it would take too many substances into consideration. For the sake of simplicity, the true oneirogens will be referred to as *oneirogens*. Alternative terms used will be *oneirogenica* or *oneiropoietica*.

Oneirogens can be classified as either natural or synthetic substances. The focus of this text will be principally on natural substances, because they generally have a more significant history of use and thus a greater depth of ethnological data. We'll also take into consideration oneirogens of animal origin, chemical compounds (endogenous and synthetic), and foods that have dream-inducing properties.

It is important to distinguish between principal oneirogens and other oneirogens. The first (principal oneirogens) are those for which there are sufficient data on their ethnobotany, chemistry, and pharmacology pointing to a possible oneirogenic effect. In the second case (other oneirogens) the data are more speculative, anecdotal, and not well referenced for lack of phytochemical and pharmacological data and human bioassays.

The data presented in this book are based not only on the available references in scientific literature but also on poorly or not referenced data and on anecdotal evidence in order to give information that is as complete as possible. We utilize a systematic, interdisciplinary research approach to oneirogens that draws on the disciplines of pharmacognosy, ethnopharmacology, ethnopharmacognosy, ethnobotany, ethnomycology, and entheobotany. (See appendix 1.)

The oneirogens considered here have been classified based upon their origins as follows:

phyto-oneirogenica: plants
myco-oneirogenica: mushrooms
zoo-oneirogenica: animals
bromato-oneirogenica: foods
oneiro-chymica: endogenous and synthetic compounds.

Oneiro-chymica comprises endo-oneirogenica (endogenous substances produced in the human body) and oneirosynthetica (synthetic drugs).

Mechanisms of Oneirogenic Action

The available data on possible oneirogen action mechanisms are very scarce. In this section we present some speculative and limited hypotheses.

Theoretically, oneirogens could act, possibly dependent on each other, in the following ways:

- increase the frequency of rapid eye movement (REM) phases in one night
- increase the duration of REM phases in one night
- increase the number of dreams in a given period of time
- modify dreams with reference to length, continuity, complexity, oddity, presence of colors, vividness, and lucidity

The increase in frequency and duration of REM phases and in the number of dreams are in relation to the sleep period. The increase in frequency and duration can occur respectively with or without an increase in the duration or frequency of the REM phases. On the other hand, the increase in the number of dreams can occur with or without an increase in frequency and/or duration of the REM phases. A related and indirect effect of oneirogens could be an improved capability of remembering dreams.

From a general point of view, the possible mechanisms of oneirogen activity could be explained by the specific actions of neurotransmitters during REM phases, in direct relation to the presence of an "oneirogenic active principle." In particular, one has to determine the following:

- if the mechanism of action is different from that of the classical hallucinogens
- if the oneirogenic active compound acts only in the dream state and/or in the waking state
- if the oneirogenic action could be prolonged and manifested throughout the night

Considering the possible actions just outlined, perhaps one has to extend and generalize the literal definition of *oneirogen* as "dream producing." Such actions could be verified by the experimental procedure of Lilian Mayagoitia presented in the next section.

Psychonautics: Evaluating Oneirogenic Activity

Psychonautics is a neologism that was first proposed by Ott to describe human experimentation with psychotropic drugs. It is derived from the word *psychonaut,* which was originally suggested in 1970 by Ernst Jünger in the seminal book *Annäherungen: Drogen and Rausch* [Approaches: Drugs and Inebriation]. In this book, Jünger documented the results of decades of pioneering research based on self-experiments with psychotropic drugs, including alcohol, opium, hashish, mescaline, LSD, and psilocybin, resulting in voyages in the inner space, which he named the "psychocosmos."

According to Ott, a psychonaut is one who travels in the universe of the mind. The term *psychonautic bioassay* refers to self-experiments with psychoactive drugs. This may be regarded by some people as a euphemism to describe new, uncontrolled, and unreported experimentations with psychoactive substances, but psychonautic bioassays are also very important sources of human pharmacological data and are invaluable in the phytochemical investigation of visionary compounds.

The psychonautic bioassay corresponds to the so-called Heffter Technique and takes its name from Dr. Arthur Heffter, who in 1897 determined with self-experiments that mescaline was the main visionary agent of the peyote cactus *(Lophophora williamsii)*, even though peyote alkaloids were isolated a decade earlier. This technique is defined as a psychonautic bioassay carried out by a scientist studying the phytochemistry or pharmacology of psychoactive plants.

The value of psychonautic bioassays was vividly demonstrated in the case of LSD. In 1938 pharmacologists working at Sandoz Pharmaceutical Company rejected LSD as a compound without pharmacological interest based on the results of their animal assays. In 1945 an intuition led Albert Hofmann to again synthesize the molecule. This experiment was followed by his well-known accidental ingestion and involuntary psychonautic bioassay, resulting in the discovery of a very potent hallucinogen. In subsequent investigations, Hofmann found that assays on animals were without significance during the isolation of active compounds from *Psilocybe mexicana* and *Turbina corymbosa*. However, Hofmann's psychonautic bioassays with *Psilocybe mexicana* and *Turbina corymbosa* helped in the discovery of psilocybin/psilocin and lysergic acid amides, respectively.

Finally, we have the case of *S. divinorum*. The active principle salvinorin A was isolated pursuant to animal assays, but it had previously been found during research on novel terpenoids. As a matter of fact, it was the so-called basement shamans who conclusively demonstrated that salvinorin A was the true visionary agent of the plant.

Ott has argued that animal bioassays have proven ineffective in some areas of research on visionary compounds and that the ethics of their use is dubious. It has been suggested by some proponents of supposedly objective double-blind animal research that psychonautic bioassays are subjective. From the ethical point of view, Ott contends that the researcher must be the first to ingest a new and putative psychoactive drug. Moreover, the following human tests must be carried out with fully informed volunteers, advised about the identity of the compound, its dose, and the effects.[4]

Ann and Alexander Shulgin recommend the use of "double-conscious" bioassays and characterize double-blind studies as pointless and possibly unethical.

The level of a substance's effects can be rated using the Shulgins' quantitative potency scale (with ratings of -, ±, +, ++, +++, ++++):

- Minus (-)There were no effects observed.
- Plus/Minus (±) The level of effectiveness of a drug that indicates a threshold action, if a higher dosage produces a greater response, then the plus/minus (±) was valid. If a higher dosage produces nothing, then the result was a false positive.
- Plus One (+) The drug is certainly active. The chronology can be determined with some accuracy, but the nature of the drug's effects is not yet apparent.
- Plus Two (++) Both the chronology and the nature of a drug are unmistakably apparent. However, you still have some choice as to whether you will accept the adventure.
- Plus Three (+++) Not only are the chronology and the nature of a drug's action quite clear, but ignoring its action is no longer an option. The subject is totally engaged in the experience.
- Plus Four (++++) A rare and precious transcendental state, which has been called a "peak experience."

The alleged dream-inducing properties of oneirogens are controversial because subjective experiences with these substances while dreaming are difficult to verify and because these subjective experiences are evasive and cannot be replicated in double-conscious human bioassays. It is difficult to evaluate if these substances act as dream-inducers in the literal sense of producing dreams, because one would need to hypothetically define and quantify an average reference characteristic of the baseline dream state for each individual. This can only be done in a very partial way, recording the main characteristics of one's dreams over a certain period of time, and then comparing them under the influence of various oneirogens.

Carrying out laboratory research on dream-inducing substances turns out to be difficult, and such research almost always yields negative results.[5] The difficulties with laboratory research pertain to the experimental setting, the expectations of the experimenter, the modality of data collection, the awakening time in relation to the different dream phases, the type of stimulus employed for the awakening, and the elaboration of the material collected.

Even though it still isn't clear that these substances actually influence oneiric production, it is true that various field researchers testify to this kind of use and that oneirogens could help us to better understand the biochemical process of dream.

A Classic Oneirogenic Experiment

The reference example for a possible objective evaluation of oneirogenic activity is represented by an experimental study carried out by Mayagoitia on the effect of extracts (hexane and methanol) of the plant *C. zacatechichi*, considered as the oneirogen of reference. The evaluations were performed on cats and humans.

In the experiments done on cats, the possible toxic behavioral effects of the two extracts at different doses were evaluated by paying attention to abnormal behaviors such as ataxia, bizarre postures, and movements toward nonexistent objects. It was noted that the cats stared for long periods of time and that, thirty minutes after the administration of the plant extracts, somnolence and sleep were frequently observed. Other behavioral effects were recorded, including salivation with vomiting, compulsive grooming, retching, bilateral contractions of nasal and maxillary muscles, and stereotyped pendulum head movements. It was not clear if some of the effects were elicited by direct central nervous system (CNS) stimulation or after local gastric irritation caused by some bitter principle contained in the plant. Several psychotropic drugs such as toluene, quipazine, and dopamine agonists can cause staring and pendular head movements, so these effects aren't specific for any one of the different classes of psychotropic compounds. Moreover, staring and pendular head movements may merely be indications of somnolence. In order to analyze more precisely the neural effects, electrophysiological recordings were taken in free-moving cats.

Various oneiromimetic compounds produced different common EEG effects in the animals. Each cat was used as its own control, and the effects of oral administration of *C. zacatechichi* extracts were compared to those of a dissociative psychodysleptic drug, such as phencyclidine, quipazine, ketamine, and SKF-10047. Both plant extracts produced similar EEG changes, which were very different from the dissociative psychodysleptic drug used, and somnolence was observed during the appearance of these changes. The results show that *C. zacatechichi* does not share the neurophysiological effects of the dissociative psychodysleptics and only induces the behavioral and EEG signs of somnolence and sleep. Given the apparently low toxicity of the plant and the ethnobotanical data, the researchers ascertained the hypnotic potency, dream-inducing effects, and other psychotropic properties in human beings.

The presence of hypnotic compounds has been detected in humans by the measurement of reaction time to a flash of light and by the subject's ability to calculate fixed time lapses. These experiments were carried out with volunteers informed about the experiment and the known effects of *C. zacatechichi,* employing active extracts and a placebo in a double-blind randomized design, where neither the volunteers nor the evaluator knew which substance had been ingested. Recorded physiological responses included EEG, electromyogram, electrocardiogram, and galvanic skin response.

No differences were found for human heart and respiratory rate, galvanic skin response, and EEG recordings. With the methanol extract, short periods of sleep (stage I) usually appeared between flash intervals when the subjects were awakened by light. Both *C. zacatechichi* extracts produced a statistically significant slowness of reaction time and an increased respiratory rate, but this change was not significantly different from controls. The characteristic EEG slowness and the increased reaction times of subjects treated with both extracts suggested that the plant might contain hypnotic compounds. Moreover, a larger effect was elicited by the methanol extract, suggesting that the active compounds might be found in the polar fractions.

EEG recordings of sleep were carried out in a similar double-blind randomized design, which, in this case, included a low dose of an active hypnotic drug (diazepam). All volunteers were asked to reduce their normal sleep time by two hours the night before testing with the extract, diazepam, or placebo. The physiological variables recorded included respiratory and heart rates, total time spent in wakefulness (W), time spent in slow-wave-sleep stages (SWS stages I to IV), and in rapid eye movement sleep (REM). Heart rate, total time, and frequency of each stage of sleep did not change with any treatment in comparison to a placebo. However, it was found that the frequency of W and SWS-IV stages were significantly modified by treatments. Post-hoc paired comparisons showed that upon onset of sleep, the methanol extract and diazepam significantly increased the frequency of W stages when compared to the placebo. In contrast, methanol extract and diazepam significantly decreased the number of SWS-IV stages. The other stages of sleep were not noticeably modified by treatment. SWS-I and SWS-II showed a slight increase in comparison to placebo, and, in contrast, SWS-III and REM stages decreased slightly. The respiratory rate was significantly modified by treatments. Paired comparisons showed that the methanol extract increased the respiratory rate when compared to all other treatments. Although this small increase may lack physiological relevance, it does suggest a pharmacological effect upon respiratory rate.

These results support the idea that *C. zacatechichi* extracts, particularly the methanol fraction, contain compounds that produce activity equivalent to sub-hypnotic diazepam doses. Ingestion of the plant produces a light hypnotic state with a decrease of both deep slow-wave sleep and REM periods.

In addition to these experimental results, the question of ethnobotanical impact on dream enhancement was evaluated by the subjective reports of the participants during the sleep study.

The psychological effects of *C. zacatechichi* extracts were evaluated by directed questionnaires and through the analysis of reports of the sensations and dreams in human volunteers. Neither the subjects, the interviewer, or the evaluator knew whether the individual had taken a plant extract, diazepam, or placebo. Significantly more dreams (in comparison to placebo) were reported for the methanol extract. Similarly, the number of dreams reported was higher following the administration of the plant extracts than with diazepam. Although not significant, the number of dreams reported was greater after the ingestion of *C. zacatechichi* extracts than placebo. The number of subjects that did not remember dreaming was always greater after placebo and diazepam administration, and, conversely, the individuals that reported more than one dream per session were always the ones treated with *C. zacatechichi* extracts. The dreams reported by subjects ingesting the plant extracts were shorter in content (measured by the number of lines written in the report). Spontaneous reports of emotions and nightmares were not different among the four treatments. Nevertheless, with the methanol extract more colors during dreaming were mentioned.

These results show that *C. zacatechichi* administration appears to enhance the number and/or recollection of dreams during sleep periods. The data are in agreement with the oneirogenic reputation of the plant among the Chontal Indians of Mexico but stand in apparent contradiction to the EEG sleep-study results. It could be expected that a compound that increases dream would also increase REM stage frequency or duration, as it has been shown to occur with physostigmine. In contrast, *C. zacatechichi* increases the stages of slow-wave sleep and apparently decreases REM sleep. This also occurs with low doses of diazepam. Despite this similarity in EEG effects, diazepam decreases dreaming reports while *C. zacatechichi* extracts enhance them. This discrepancy may be explained by the fact that dreaming and sleep imagery are not restricted to REM episodes but also occur during slow-wave sleep (SWS

I and II) when lively hypnagogic images are reported as brief dreams. All this suggests that *C. zacatechichi* induces episodes of lively hypnagogic imagery during slow-wave stage I sleep, a psychophysiological effect that would be the basis of the ethnobotanical use of the plant as an oneirogenic and oneiromantic agent.

Considering that *C. zacatechichi* is the prototype of the oneirogens and the most studied in this class of substances, along with the fact that there are substantial ethnobotanical data for this substance, it is possible to consider the evaluation method of Mayagoitia as the reference method in the evaluation of the activity of oneirogens in general, but limited to human bioassays. On the basis of the effects registered for *C. zacaechichi,* the parameters to be evaluated for the effect of an oneirogen in comparison to a placebo can be summarized as follows:

- respiratory rate
- EEG
- frequency of SWS-I, SWS-II, SWS-III and SWS-IV stages of sleep
- REM sleep stage periods
- hypnagogic phenomena during SWS-I
- directed questionnaires and analysis of reports of the subjective sensations and dreams, including number and recollection of dreams, length, and presence of colors

Such a method could be applied to a variety of possible oneirogenic substances, starting with those that have extensive ethnobotanical, phytochemical, and pharmacological literature. Human bioassays are very important in studying oneirogens, especially if undertaken in the same traditional context in which they are normally employed. Carrying out "in field" autoexperimentations among peoples who use such substances could give us a better understanding of the meaning of the induced oneiric experience.

2

A History of Dream

From the beginning of civilization, dreams have regulated the lives of people in relation with each other and with divinity. Dreams have had a cultural and social importance particularly in ancient civilizations, in non-Western cultures, and above all in the cultures of illiterate populations.

For the primitive mentality, the visible and the invisible world are viewed as the same thing, with a constant interchange occurring between physical reality and mystical forces. This interchange is ideally achieved in the dream state. Primitives believed only in sensorial experiences. As a result, they tended to interpret the fantastic dimension of dreams in terms of reality, conferring an actual meaning to dreams, and accepting as truth the facts represented by dreams. In this way, the invisible world was seen as part of individual and social reality. As a result, for primitive societies the dream could be a means of knowledge of a sacred external reality. The dream itself was seen as a potently creative and transforming human experience.

In archaic societies, the oneiromancy (interpretation of dreams) and oneiropoietic practices (induction of dreams) were established as cultural institutions related to the individual and collective destiny and endowed with religious meaning. Dreams, myths, and rites were interconnected; the cultural element was part of the psychic element and the reverse. Among illiterate peoples and in some ancient world cultures, the dream was linked to myth, mostly to the "myths of origin." Dream was seen as a means for returning to the creativity of origins, just as every society finds in myth the model of its culture. In the same way, every person finds the model of personal destiny in dream.

In the anthropological literature on dreams and dreaming among primitive peoples, the focus of study is on what Barbara Herr referred to in 1981 as the "ethnography of dreams." There is very little recent research on the ethnography of dreams among primitive peoples in anthropology. A classic study on the ethnography of dreams by Marie Reay was published in 1962, in which she describes dreams among primitive people as *sweet* witchcraft, a form of good magic.

Ancient Theories on the Origin and Interpretation of Dreams

In the ancient Mediterranean, the dream was always linked to religion (and then to the invisible world), but it was perceived as distinct from reality, in contrast with primitive thought. This represents the beginning of the interpretation of dreams as we know it. The ancient Egyptians were perhaps the first people to understand the importance of the language of dreams, the narrative and formal aspects of dreams, and the use of dreams to learn the cause of diseases and how to cure them (dream incubation).

Generally, in the ancient world dreams were considered to have been sent by a divine agent. They were classified as either true (as an admonition or a prediction of the future) or false (to divert or trick).

The Greeks found dreams to be particularly important. Starting from a more ancient tradition, the Greeks attributed an obscure origin to dreams, believing that they originated beyond the ocean, beyond the limits of the cosmos. The dream world was identified with the mythical era of origin, the epoch during which all forms were created from chaos. The myths of origin were related to social life, while dreams were related to the individual life and personal destiny. In practice, dreaming was seen as a means for renewing the union with mythical origins by means of the ancestors. Ancestors, heroes, and the dead magically guided the events of the waking state.

In ancient Greece, the Oracle at Delphi in honor of the god Apollo was a source of divinitation about the future through prophecies, visions, and the interpretation of dreams. The Delphic Oracle was a woman who would enter a trancelike state and experience visions and dreams that the ancient Greeks consulted for information about the future. James F. Johnston in 1857 suggested that the prophecies of the Delphic Oracle were associated with the use of psychoactive plants that were similar to those used by South American Indians, for example, *Brugmansia*. This suggestion seems unlikely, as *Brugmansia* species are native only to South America. It was recently discovered, however, that the Delphic Oracle may have inhaled the vapors of ethylene gas that were emitted from limestone rocks in the caves where she was visited by people from throughout ancient Greece. The limestone caves where the Delphic Oracle lived have been shown to emit high concentrations of ethylene gas. It is now known that ethylene vapors have an effect on the central nervous system capable of producing visions and dreams.

Among the best-known Greek scholars interested in dreams were Aristotle and his followers, who proposed a psychophysiological interpretation of sleep and dreams. Aristotle affirms that dreams aren't sent by the gods, that they aren't of divine nature at all, but are demonic in origin, because nature itself is demonic. This means that dreams aren't supernatural manifestations but that they follow the rules of the human spirit, even if that spirit is similar to the divine nature. So dreams are defined as the activity of the sleeping person. Aristotle also believed that dreams could reveal the symptoms of some diseases, as did Hippocrates.

Another Greek, Strato of Lampasco, hypothesized that sleep originated by a withdrawal of the sensations, a very modern concept. Artemidorus of Daldi, and then Macrobius, systematically classified dreams in a manner close to that of modern psychology. Artemidorus could be considered a precursor of psychoanalysis in his attempt to systematize the oneiric symbols and their meaning.

Dream incubation (oneiric oracle) had a great therapeutic importance in ancient Greece and was propitiated in the sanctuary of Apollo or Asclepius. The remedies obtained in dream came in natural forms or in symbols and images interpreted by priests. Aristides gave great importance to dream incubation, personally receiving in his own dreams the therapeutic practices to be carried out on a patient. Dream incubation was also a technique followed by Christian hermits.

To Plato dreams were indicative of possible pathological conditions (hallucinations or delirium caused by mental or physical diseases). The philosopher wasn't interested in the dream phenomena, excluding its sacred value and the value of the possible truth hidden in it. Plato's ideas have remained isolated.

From the Late Greek epoch through the following centuries books of dreams were addressed to more learned persons, especially the work of Nicephorus, patriarch of Constantinople. Likewise, in early medieval times the interpretation of dreams was directed mostly to kings and emperors.

In late medieval times the dream was considered a means by which the common man could evade reality and express himself in an imaginary world. The idea that dreams had an oracular meaning was also common. To pagans, dreams were sent by the gods, while for Christians, they were sent by God, angels, and saints. In the pagan world dreams were interpreted as true or false, while in the Middle Ages they were seen as divine or diabolical. As a result, very ancient practices (such as dream incubation) and pagan beliefs could coexist with the contemplative, meditative, and prophetic aspects of the Christian religion. As a Christian, Tertullianus was the first to formulate a "theology of dream." According to him, the visions experienced in dreams can lead to the knowledge of God and of oneself. Dreams can be deceiving (sent by Satan) or true (sent by God). A similar interpretation is that of Clement Alexandrinus. He affirms that dreaming is a moral metaphor for a specific spiritual state, different from man to man. For Saint Augustine dream idealizes the omnipotence of God and reveals it to man, but he did not see dreams as always being the way to reach the Truth.

By the twelfth century the dream experience was no longer interpreted as a representation of a cosmological order identified with God but as a human event to be rationalized. We remember John of Salisbury and Pascal Romanus. John of Salisbury proposed the idea that the same dream could have different meanings, while Pascal Romanus theorized that a dream could give a correct medical diagnosis, therefore putting dream into the field of the natural sciences and taking it out of the field of magic. For Romanus the dream hides cognitions manifested in symbols and metaphors to be interpreted, so the dream becomes a private experience with an individual psychological meaning.

Modern Theories on the Origin of Dreams

For the ancient people there was no need to search for dream stimuli, because dreams were sent by the gods. But in recent centuries science has been asked to explain if there was a stimulus to dream. In practice this meant determining if the causes were psychological or physiological.

Sigmund Freud was sceptical toward the interpretation of dreams as messages from an occult world. He was also unwilling to accept the theory that the individual psyche has access to a whole range of dream images (archetypes) common to all persons (the collective unconscious). For Freud the dream is a model for the formation of the unconscious; the oneiric work aims to hide and distort buried elements.

Freud, in *Die Traumdeutung (The Interpretation of Dreams)* (1900), discusses the origin of dreams. According to his theory, dreams are the consequence (a reaction) to troubled sleep.

Freud proposed that dream could be caused by any of the following stimuli:

- external sensory excitations (objective)
- internal sensory excitations (subjective)
- internal physical stimuli (organic)
- psychic stimuli

In the first case, he proposed a correspondence between the external sensory stimuli (caused by the environmental conditions during sleep and noted at waking) and a part of the dream content; these stimuli can be confirmed. On the contrary, the subjective internal sensory excitation sources (for example, hypnagogic phenomena) cannot be easily confirmed.

Internal physical stimuli (organic) are the third of Freud's proposed dream stimuli. In the waking state, we are conscious of a diffused, general sensitiveness, a vague quality we call mood. Such sensation is determined by all of our organic components. According to Freud's theory, during sleep the mind (being estranged from the external world) can pay more attention to the interior of the body. These internal organic stimuli can induce excitations that could be transformed into oneiric images, though such stimuli are not indispensable for dream production.

The oneiric images can also be related to the malfunctioning of our physical organs. A researcher cited by Freud experimentally confirmed this possibility. For example, those who suffer from heart or lung disease or have digestive problems would have dreams with a content that represent such physical diseases in a more or less direct and symbolic way. The organic stimuli can pertain to the general sensitiveness and the specific vegetative sensations (muscular, respiratory, gastric, sexual, and peripheral). According to the dream generation process reported by Freud, the awakened sensation evokes a similar image by means of some associative principle, combining with it in an organic structure. In particular, if one of our organs is excited as a consequence of the external action of an emotional state, then the dream will contain images related to that emotional state. Thus the psychic stimuli work in cooperation with the physical ones. The psychic stimuli are due to the nervous excitation and mental associations.

In the end, according to Freud, the dream can be considered to be the result of a physiological stimulus expressed in psychic symptoms. In the case of oneirogens, dreams could originate by means of an external excitation (taking the oneirogen) that manifests its effect internally with an action involving neurotransmitters and receptors.

In the modern Western world the importance attributed to dreams in primitive societies and the ancient world is now substituted by scientific and analytical knowledge. This scientific and analytical knowledge includes philosophy, psychology, psychoanalysis, ethnology, and sociology. Primitive peoples and ancient societies regarded dreams and dreaming as sacred and magical, and the Western world continues to be fascinated by dreams and dreaming. But in modern times dreams have lost the cultural and social importance they had in the ancient world. Now dreams are linked to the practice of psychoanalysis as an important means in the study of the unconscious. However, it seems that they have lost their sacredness and in today's modern Western world, interest in dreams and dreaming is a profane and secular means for introspection and self-consciousness.

3

The Oneirocosmos

Sleep and Dream Chemistry

Sleep is a neurophysiological and neurochemical state characterized by an almost total interruption of external sensory perceptions. It is also dependent upon a psychological internal component defined by environmental and sociocultural factors, which influences the content of dreams. The physiological processes of the sleep mechanism are regulated by environmental conditions (light levels and temperature), the light/darkness cycle, mood (hormonal) variations, body temperature, and genetic factors.

One of the primary tools for the scientific study of sleep and dreams is the electroencephalogram, or EEG. During the waking state, the EEG tracing describes a rapid course with an irregular frequency; this is the de-synchronized cerebral state of activation. Passing from relaxation to the sleeping state, the EEG tracing has a slower course; this is the synchronized cerebral state of repose.

There are five sleep phases. The first corresponds to falling asleep and is characterized by a decrease of alpha waves and the appearance of theta waves, a slight drop of muscular tone, the absence of rapid eye movement, and, sometimes, a mental state similar to dream. In the second phase, the EEG rhythms are ulteriorly slowed down, with prevalence of theta waves and an absence of rapid eye movement. In the third and fourth phases, delta waves appear and the absence of rapid eye movement persists.

Some ninety minutes after falling asleep, the fourth phase is interrupted and the EEG tracing becomes paradoxically de-synchronized as in the waking state, while the subject remains asleep. This is the fifth phase. Such activity defines the REM (or paradoxical) sleep phase, characterized by the presence of PGO (ponto-genicolo-occipital) waves and rapid eye movement. REM phases increase in duration throughout the night, with the longer ones corresponding to that of morning, or the period before awakening.

REM sleep is considered to be the neurophysiological basis for dream. Rapid eye movement is thought to be the motor equivalent of a hallucinatory activity in the creation of the oneiric space, while the PGO waves are the electric expression of the decodification of the information in the central nervous system (CNS), experienced as visual hallucinations. J. Allan Hobson and Robert W. McCarley have formulated the so-called internal generator theory, which proposes that the brain in the REM state is a generator of the dream state. According to these researchers, the REM state inhibits sensorial input and internally stimulates the brain, producing information then elaborated in specific cerebral areas. In practice, the main origin of the dream state would be physiological.

However, evidence seems to deny the REM phase being the exclusive internal generator of dream. The mental activity while falling asleep and in the non-REM phases is not easily distinguishable from that of REM sleep. In non-REM phases, mental activity could be more conceptual, with fragments of thought and reflections linked to daily experiences, without hallucinations and with scarce emotive participation.

Oneiric experiences are produced in all phases of the non-REM and REM sleep, but only in the REM phases does the cerebral activation permit the memory to recover. So it is possible to hypothesize a single system for oneiric production throughout the sleep cycle.

The fact that sleep-inducing compounds have been identified in the CNS has led to the hypothesis that sleep is due to the accumulation of these compounds in the brain. In practice various activities during the waking state can induce the production of different endogenous substances; they activate different neuronal groups responsible for the distinct phases of sleep.

According to this neurochemical hypothesis of sleep, different neurotransmitters are involved in the production and maintenance of the sleep phases and the waking state. The neurotransmitters are as follows:

acetylcholine	catecholamines
melatonin	histamine
gamma-aminobutyric acid	adenosine
serotonin	nitrous oxide

Acetylcholine

Among the neurotransmitters involved in the induction and maintenance of REM sleep, surely acetylcholine merits attention. It is a very important compound in the control of the waking state and REM sleep. The activation of the cholinergic neurons (those relative to acetylcholine) of the pons is responsible for the induction and maintenance of REM sleep. Such activation is possible as a consequence of the reduction in the aminergic and serotonergic inhibition.

Acetylcholine binds to the muscarinic receptors, in particular M_1, M_2, and M_3. The M_1 receptors are important in maintaining REM sleep but not in inducing it. The M_2 receptors regulate the sleep phases and induce and maintain REM sleep, while the M_3 receptors control the alternation of the waking and non-REM phases but without modifying REM sleep.

Melatonin

Melatonin regulates physiological changes related to light, time of day, and other factors. It is produced by the pineal gland. Melatonin's synthesis is inhibited by light, so it reaches higher concentrations during the night and lower concentrations during the day.

Gamma-Aminobutyric Acid (GABA)

Gamma-aminobutyric acid is the most important and widespread inhibitory neurotransmitter in the brain. GABA is able to induce relaxation, analgesia, and sleep. It has a role in the induction of synchronous sleep (particularly the gabaergic neurons of the preoptic areas). But GABA can also inhibit the serotonergic neurons of the dorsal raphe, so inducing REM sleep.

Serotonin (5-HT)

Produced by the neurons of the raphe, serotonin is an essential neurotransmitter in the physiological processes leading to sleep.

Several serotonin receptors have been identified, along with their subtypes. The activity of the serotonergic neurons of the raphe is at a maximum during the waking state and diminishes during non-REM sleep, reaching a minimum during REM sleep.

It has been hypothesized that serotonin is set free during the waking state and that it induces the synthesis and release of other compounds responsible for the sleep state. It is also possible that serotonin increases cerebral metabolic activity during the waking state, lowering glycogen in the brain, which in turn causes an increase of adenosine and a consequent EEG synchronization and sleep, so permitting a new synthesis of glycogen and assisting the metaboliv recovery of the nervous system during sleep.

Catecholamines

Generally, noradrenalin and dopamine produce and maintain the waking state. The noradrenergic neurons of the locus coeruleus could be involved in the appearance of REM sleep. In fact, such neurons (as the serotonergic ones of the raphe) have inhibitory control over the cholinergic neurons of the pons, involved in the production of REM phases.

Histamine

The histaminergic neurons are found in the hypothalamic nuclei and regulate the waking state. The H_1 receptors for histamine are involved in the effects of this neurotransmitter on the sleep/waking cycle.

Adenosine

Adenosine seems to participate in the induction and maintenance of non-REM and REM sleep, interacting with two receptors, A_1 and A_2. Adenosine is accumulated during the waking state, increasing the conductance of potassium in the thalamic and cortical neurons and leading to EEG synchronization and sleep. Adenosine also has an inhibitory action on the noradrenergic and cholinergic neurons of the trunk, involved in the waking state. The production of adenosine would be a consequence of the lowering of glycogen, so favoring the metabolic recovery of the nervous system by means of sleep.

There are other substances whose release during the waking state is accompanied by a lowering in the concentration of cerebral glycogen and the production of adenosine. These substances are serotonin, noradrenalin, histamine, and the vasoactive intestinal polypeptide.

Nitrous Oxide

It seems that this gas plays a role in the modulation of the synaptic activities in the CNS and is possibly involved in sleep modulation. This gas could also mediate the ipnogenic effect of interleukin-1 (a cytokine), which induces an increase in the concentration of nitrous oxide.

The mechanism of dream is rather complex, involving different neurotransmitters, cerebral areas, and sleep phases. Even if the neurochemical studies are in constant development, our understanding of the dream process remains limited.

4
Phyto-Oneirogenica
Plants

We don't know exactly how many plant species are employed for psychoactive purposes around the world, but surely many species have yet to be discovered or identified. Almost all cultures have discovered and employed psychoactive species, even in those areas where such species are less abundant. The numbers are higher in the New World in respect to the Old World, but the reason is not a botanical one. Instead, we have to think of a cultural reason.

In the New World there were visionary shamanic cultures that still exist today, for which the experience of the altered states of consciousness is a common practice and a means of human expression. Such societies could be considered culturally programmed for the search and use of psychoactive species. On the other hand, the dogmatic religions of the Old World erased or transformed ancient cults that contrasted with the new beliefs. Such cults became taboo or were linked to the devil.

Among the effects reported for a great variety of species, the oneirogenic action seems the most evanescent and difficult to study; at the same time it could have a special importance for traditional use.

In the following pages we take a detailed look at the wide variety of plants included in the phyto-oneirogenica category.

Ayahuasca

Ayahuasca is a hallucinogenic beverage of Amazonia essentially prepared with the liana *Banisteriopsis caapi* and other plants containing N,N-dimethyltryptamine (DMT), such as *B. rusbyana, Diplopterys cabrerana,* and *Psychotria viridis,* along with many other additives. It is known as *yagé, natema,* and *caapi.*

It is not our intent to precisely discuss preparations and uses for ayahuasca. It is sufficient to say here that the beverage is widely used and has great importance among natives. It is a vital part of the social life of the users and of their mythical tales, but only shamans are allowed to make and use it.

It is employed in curing and religious ceremonies, for divination, and in recognizing dangers. Ayahuasca induces a powerful visionary state allowing shamans to see gods, the first human beings, animals, and to understand the establishment of tribal social order. In some ceremonies the Indians ingest the beverage during the night, because the effects are stronger in the dark and the dreams produced are more abundant.

B. caapi contains β-carbolines such as harmine, harmaline, and harmol, which are also present in different plant species, such as Syrian rue *(Peganum harmala).* They are monoamine oxidase inhibitors (MAOI). The enzyme monoamine oxidase is widely distributed in human tissues, and it is important for the metabolism of endogenous neurotransmitters in the human brain, including dopamine, noradrenalin, and 5-hydroxytryptamine (serotonin). DMT isn't active when ingested alone, because MAO enzymes degrade it. On the contrary, DMT is active when taken orally in combination with an MAOI compound, because the compound inactivates the MAO enzymes. In this way, DMT passes unaltered through the blood-brain barrier and manifests its effect.

Brugmansia spp.

These plants were already being cultivated in pre-Columbian times by Indians of South America. They are known by the names *huacacachu, chamico, floripondio, toa, campanilla, maicoa,* and *borrachero.* The leaves are used to make visionary narcotic drinks. In the resulting ecstatic state the subject can speak to the spirits of the ancestors, contact the gods, and get information on hidden treasures. The dried leaves are added to tobacco *(Nicotiana rustica)* and smoked by the Tzeltal Indians of Mexico. In this way they enter into a visionary state and undertake curing actions. Species of *Brugmansia* are also additives in ayahuasca.

The scent of the flowers is also psychoactive. It is reported from Mexico that the fresh flowers induce a deep sleep and beautiful erotic dreams. The plant is also used as an aphrodisiac and in medicine to cure respiratory problems, wounds, and tumors.

The plant causes delirium accompanied by hypnagogic phenomena and hallucinations. It contains scopolamine and atropine.

Calea zacatechichi

This plant surely represents the best-known oneirogen prototype. Known in the United States as *dream herb*, in Aztec language *(nahuatl) zacate-chichi* means "bitter herb." Another ancient Aztec name associated with the plant is *cozticzapotl* ("fruit that makes unsteady"), also attributable to the species *Casimiroa edulis* and *Lucuma salicifolia. C. zacatechichi* was believed to be employed by Aztec sorcerers *(nagualli)* in order to travel more rapidly to Tlalocan, the region of dreams.

C. zacatechichi can be found from Mexico to Costa Rica. It is used by the Chontal Indians of Oaxaca, Mexico, among whom the plant is known as *zacatechichi* and *thle-pelakano* ("leaf of the god") as well as *zacate de perro* ("herb of the dog") and *hoja madre* ("mother leaf").

It is believed that the plant purifies the senses and that the visions induced in dreams mold the future or help in foretelling it. The more important use of this oneirogen is for obtaining divinatory messages in the dream state, for example to learn the origin of an illness or the place where a distant or lost person can be found.

The prescribed quantity is "a handful" of dried leaves. The crushed leaves are smoked or drunk in a water infusion. Generally, after slowly drinking the infusion, the person lies down in a quiet place and smokes a cigarette made with more leaves. Still more leaves are placed under the pillow before going to sleep. The use of a sufficient quantity is confirmed by a sensation of peacefulness, nausea, somnolence, and the reduction of one's pulsations and heartbeats, in addition to subtle auditive changes.

This oneirogenic practice induces lucid, vivid, or significant dreams. It is also reported to induce an expansion of all the sensory perceptions and imagination, a slight discontinuity of thought, a rapid flux of ideas, and difficulty in remembering. According to some, there is a visual effect; according to others, an auditive one wherein the plant speaks to the person. Generally a sensation of well-being lasting one day or more is common.

It doesn't appear that *C. zacatechichi* always produces oneirogenic activity, perhaps because, according to the Chontal Indians, only certain specimens of the plant are active. In fact, they distinguish between "good" and "bad" varieties according to whether they have or do not have psychoactive properties. This fact proves that distinct samples have shown differences in chemical composition.

C. zacatechichi has been employed since ancient times against fever, colics, gastrointestinal disorders, diarrhea, and cholera. It is also used as an aperitif and insecticide. In Yucatan the leaves are used to treat skin eruptions.

Until now, no psychoactive compound has been identified, but triterpenes, sesquiterpenic lactones, a glycoside, and an alkaloid with a possible light psychoactive effect have been isolated; another compound found in the leaves has a depressive effect on the CNS. The main identified compounds include calaxine, ciliarine, zacatechinolides, caleocromane A and B, caleine A and B, and caleicine I and II. The plant is used as a substitute for *Cannabis sativa*.

Casimiroa edulis

Known in ancient times as *cozticzapotl* ("fruit that makes unsteady") and in modern times as *zapote blanco* ("white zapote"), *zapote borracho* ("drunken zapote"), and *zapote dormilón* ("narcotic zapote"), this species was employed by the Aztecs as a narcotic in the form of seed ash. Today, in traditional Mexican medicine, a tea is prepared with the leaves in order to counteract troubled sleep and for regulating and stimulating dreams. The Tzotzil Indians of Mexico take the bark extract as an ecbolic.

The seeds contain N-benzoiltyramine, methylhistamine, casimiroine, casimiroidine, fagarine, and scopoletine, while the leaves contain methylhistamine, dimethylhistamine, and rutine. The plant might contain traces of DMT.

Clematis virginiana

It is reported that the Iroquois Indians of North America employed a decoction of stems of this species in order to induce "strange dreams," and other hallucinogenic effects.

Relevant biochemical data are not available, even though in other genera of the same family of *C. virginiana,* and in particular in *Clematis* spp., toxic alkaloids have been identified. Some species of *Clematis* contain skin irritant compounds (such as anemonine), which when ingested cause the mouth to burn. The Nez Percé Indians of North America employ *C. hirsutissima* as horse stimulant, putting the cleaned roots in the animal's nostrils, probably exploiting the local irritant effect of anemonine. In earlier times in Bavaria the shoots of *C. vitalba* were used as an additive in smoking tobacco (*Nicotiana* sp.).

Cymbopogon densiflorus

It seems that this tropical plant is employed by the sorcerers of the Central African Republic and by the shamans of Tanganyika, who call the plant *esakuna.* The shamans smoke the leaves or flowers, alone or in a mixture with tobacco. It is used as a substitute for *C. sativa* in order to induce divinatory dreams and to predict the future.

In Tanganyika the leaves and rhizomes are known for their tonic and astringent properties. The plant is also known in the Congo, Gabon, and Malawi.

There isn't specific data for the presence of active compounds. The species could be infested by parasitic mushrooms, thus producing psychoactive ergot alkaloids. The genus is rich in essential oils, and the leaves and rhizomes of *C. densiflorus* have a lemon scent.

Cypripedium calceolus

This orchid was gathered in sacred bundles by the Menominee Indians of North America and used for inducing "supernatural dreams," while the Cherokee Indians used it for its sedative, stimulant, analgesic, and anticonvulsive properties. For the American colonists it was a substitute for valerian *(Valeriana officinalis),* used against irritability, hysteria, and insomnia.

Scarce data lead to a hypothesis of potential psychoactivity, not only as an oneirogen but also more specifically as a hallucinogen. Cipripedine and a quinone analogue have been identified, along with irritant compounds, but there is no proof of the presence of psychoactive compounds.

Desfontainia spinosa

D. spinosa has a wide geographical distribution, from Costa Rica to the Andes, from Colombia to Chile, but it is one of the lesser-known Andean plants. It is used as an oneirogenic species in diagnoses among shamans of the Kamsá tribe in the Sibundoy Valley in Colombia, where it is called *borrachero de páramo* ("inebriant of the inhospitable land"). Kamsá shamans prepare a tea with *D. spinosa* leaves or fruits when they wish to have dreams, visions, or to diagnose illnesses. The beverage can be so potent that, according to an informant, it can drive one mad. It is employed infrequently, and only in the most difficult cases. The inhaled smoke of the leaves has a psychoactive effect.

In Chile it is called *chapico, michai blanco, taique,* and *trautrau.* It is known as an inebriant, as the variety *D. spinosa* var. *hookerii*. The Mapuche shamans of Chile *(machis)* employ it for its psychoactive properties (narcotic ones), against stomachache, and as yellow dye. In the folklore of Chiloè (island of south Chile), there is a mythological being called El Trauco, representing the primary spirit of *trautrau* in the form of a perverse little being, a satyr of the forest.

Biochemical information is still scarce, but the plant could contain alkaloids because it is closely linked with the Loganiaceae family, which is rich in alkaloids.

Duboisia hopwoodii

D. hopwoodii occurs throughout the arid regions and sandy soils of Australia. The plant is used in various contexts by the Aborigines of Australia and occasionally by other ethnic groups who call it *pituri*. This name refers also to plants chewed or smoked by the Aborigines for hedonistic or magical purposes, especially species of tobacco and *Datura* sp.

The most important use of the plant is for psychoactive purposes. Procuring and processing these substances requires much skill, knowledge, and labor. In fact, aboriginal production, distribution, and consumption of *D. hopwoodii* seems to demonstrate culturally controlled drug use in its most historically tested form. Only the male elders knew where to find pituri plants, and younger men and women were not allowed to accompany the elders while they harvested the plant. Techniques used in the preparation of pituri were a jealously guarded secret among male elders who also controlled its distribution within the community. The great significance of *D. hopwoodii* is evident by the fact that those who were in possession of the plant could buy anything with it. The plant was gathered for use during long, arduous expeditions and was traded with neighboring groups. Such trade was monopolized by the clans whose ancestors first discovered the effects of the plant and then developed the methods of preparation.

The preparation of pituri followed a precise ritual. Old men prepared a fire. They then created a hole in the fire by raking away the coals down to the hot sand. The branch tips of *D. hopwoodii* were cut, placed in the hole, and cooked for roughly two hours. The sand was raked off, and the plant was cooled, dried, and then beaten. The big twigs were discarded while the smaller clean ones were gathered in a bag. The plant was consumed much like chewing tobacco. The leaves were combined with alkali from the ash of *Acacia salicina* in order to release the active principle (nicotine). It seems that the use of pituri disappeared after the colonization of Australia.

Pituri probably wasn't part of the religious beliefs of the Aborigines; instead, it was used for its stimulant properties, allowing people to work for a longer time, suppress hunger and thirst, and travel for long distances. During social gatherings pituri was passed from mouth to mouth, promoting fellowship and mirth. It also has an inebriating effect.

There is an unsubstantiated report that *D. hopwoodii* has been used by Australian Aborigines in ritual killings. In central Australia *D. hopwoodii* is used in hunting to poison emus, kangaroos, wallabies, parrots, and other birds. Emus that drink the poisoned water quickly become stupefied and are easily killed or die from the effects of the poison.

It is reported that the plant produces visions, pleasant and passionate dreams, or nightmares. This oneirogenic property may have some relationship to the concept of the "dreamtime" in aboriginal magic.

The plant contains nicotine, nornicotine (four times more toxic than nicotine), piturine, and duboisine with stimulating and toxic effects. The concentrations of nicotine and nornicotine vary widely from plant to plant, so an individual plant could serve as either a stimulant or a narcotic.

Anecdotal reports of the oneirogenic properties of nicotine or nicotine-containing products (such as tobacco or pharmaceutical nicotine preparations) agree with the presumed oneirogenic activity of *D. hopwoodii*. In fact, nicotine has a cholinergic action that could induce oneiric production.

Other nicotine-containing plants are *Acacia retinoides, Arum maculatum, Asclepias syriaca, Cestrum* spp., *Cyphomandra* spp., *Datura metel, Duboisia myoporoides, Equisetum palustre, Erythroxylon* spp., *Mucuna pruriens,* and, above all, species of *Nicotiana* (principally *N. rustica* and *N. tabacum*).

Elaeagnus sp.

In Papua New Guinea an unidentified *Elaeagnus* species has been added to tobacco and smoked to produce a trance or dreamlike oneirogenic state by the Gimi of the Eastern Highlands. Under the name of "mistletoe," *Elaeagnus* sp. is also a component of psychoactive smoking mixtures used among numerous Native Americans. These mixtures are known as *kinnikinnik* and contain tobacco.

Several species contain β-carboline alkaloids, including *Elaeagnus angustifolia, E. hortensis, E. orientalis,* and *E. spinosa.* In particular harmaline has been isolated from *E. angustifolia,* while tetrahydroharmine is a constituent of *E. hortensis, E. orientalis,* and *E. spinosa.* Harman is the most common natural β-carboline alkaloid and is found in at least forty-five plant species in thirteen different families. It is especially common in the Passifloraceae and Rubiaceae families.

Compounds like β-carboline alkaloids (harmine and harmaline) have psychoactive properties. These alkaloids are not pyrolyzed during smoking and are known to produce a sedative effect similar to diazepam (Valium).

Considering the data reported for *D. hopwoodii* and other nicotine-containing plants, it is possible that the oneirogenic effect ascribed to *Elaeagnus* sp. is due to the presence of nicotine in tobacco or that its active principles modulate the effect of nicotine. It is also possible that *Elaeagnus* sp. has an oneirogenic effect by itself.

Entada rheedii

This plant is found from South Africa to tropical Africa, in India, Asia, and Australia. Its very large seeds frequently wash up on beaches along the African coast ("sea beans").[1]

Entada rheedi is known as "African dream herb," and tobacco made from the seeds has been used to help induce vivid dreaming. In an autoexperimentation, the powdered nutmeat of the seed was mixed with *N. rustica*. There were slight hallucinations, color sensations, and very strange dreams.

The seeds have various medicinal uses, as an ointment to treat jaundice, and are also worn on necklaces and pendants as lucky charms. No psychoactive compounds have been identified in this species.

Erythrina americana

Erythrina spp. are tropical and subtropical species of both hemispheres. They are known in Mexico as *sinicuiche* (name given principally to *Heimia salicifolia*), while the seeds are known as *colorines* or *chilicote*. The use of the plant as an entheogen is not well established. It is known that the Aztecs used the seeds of some species as an inebriant.

As for *E. americana,* prophets and magicians of the Ixil and Mam Indian ethnic groups of Guatemala used the seeds of the plant for divination in order to communicate with spirits; while the Yucatan Maya Indians invoked the tree (the *tzompanquahuitl* of the Aztecs, a tree linked to sacrificial death) as a magical remedy. Moreover the Aztecs used the wood of the plant to represent their gods. Today the wood and the seeds are sold as protective amulets in Mexico.

The beans supposedly have aphrodisiac properties (turning women into nymphomaniacs), inducing ecstatic madness, dreams, and possible death. The plant and particularly the seeds contain erythrane alkaloids such as erythrane, erythroidin, corallin, coralloidin, and erythro-coralloidin, producing effects similar to that of curare and cytisine. The presence of cytisine is also reported.

Other species have various uses. *E. flabelliformis* is employed as a remedy by the Tarahumara Indians of Mexico, *E. glauca* and *E. poeppigiana* are used as purgative ayahuasca additives *(amacisa).*

Galbulimima belgraveana

This is a species of the Pacific rain forests, widespread in Papua New Guinea, Indonesia, and Australia. The following data are relative to Papua New Guinea.

In the Okapa region of the Eastern Highlands this tree is known as *agara*. The natives eat or boil the leaves and the aromatic bark along with the leaves of a not well-identified species of *Homalomena* (probably *Homalomena belgraveana, H. ereriba* or *H. lauterbachii*), called *ereriba*.

In 1957 the Australian dietician Lucy Hamilton, along with French ethnobotanist Jacques Barrau, conducted an experiment at Okapa to observe the effects of eating agara bark. A local man called Ogia volunteered for the experiment. Seven or eight pieces of agara bark about the "size of a penny" were masticated and ingested. While Ogia masticated, he also smoked some tobacco, chewed some ginger (*Zingiber* sp.), and ate dried leaves of ereriba. When Ogia finished masticating the bark, it was ingested and he waited for the effect. Hamilton reports that the effects began a few minutes later.

He began to tremble like a "kuru meri" (the Melanesian Pidgin term for a woman affected by the serious neurological disorder kuru, with symptoms resembling Parkinson's disease). Then the trembling ceased and he became violent. He picked up a stick and chased several people. Hamilton was convinced that such behavior was not an act. The subject neither spoke nor smiled and at first he seemed not to hear. The pupils of his eyes were pinpoints.[2]

This destructive frenzy was followed by calmness, euphoria, drowsiness, and finally deep sleep that lasted for several hours. It has been suggested that after eating agara bark visions are experienced while asleep. These visions are reported to be of men or animals to be killed. For this reason, agara bark was known as "dream man" among the Fore people in the Eastern Highlands province. The term *dream man* is derived from the Melanesian Pidgin (Tok Pisin) word *driman,* which means "dream." It also refers to several other substances used by the Fore to produce visions, including ereriba and *maraba* (*Kaempferia galanga* rhizome).

Ogia reported no visions, and later he told Hamilton that the reason that he did not experience any visions was because he did not want to. It was also suggested to Hamilton that in this experiment Ogia had eaten the bark in the morning and not in the evening, which was thought to be the proper time to eat "dream man."

The Gimi of the Eastern Highlands employ *G. belgraveana* alone in order to foresee the future and induce visionary and trance states as well as to hinder the evil powers that cause illness. In the latter case, the *aona bana* ("man of power") chews the bark in order to induce a trance state and contact the *aona* ("attendant spirit") of the patient, obtaining information about the disease condition and the future. In the same province, leaves and bark are employed for stimulating aggressiveness and courage in young persons.

Among the people of Aseki (the southern part of Morobe Province, Papua New Guinea), the bark *(waga)* is used as an analgesic after being chewed, spit, having salt added to it, and finally ingested. The Oksapmin of the western Sepik Province mix the minced bark with wild ginger (*Zingiber* sp.), obtaining the *alusa*. It counteracts the effects of sorcery, including skin diseases, fever, and poisonings. The Bimin-Kiskusmin, found in the western Sepik Province, have also employed this plant ritual.

Benjamin Thomas carried out a psychonautical bioassay. The results are as follows:

7:15 p.m.	10 grams of dried and powdered agara bark masticated for ten minutes
7:16 p.m.	Intensely bitter taste
7:20 p.m.	Strong alkaloidal aftertaste similar to quinine
7:25 p.m.	Bark swallowed
7:55 p.m.	Alert, becoming drowsy
7:57 p.m.	Dilated pupils
8:00 p.m.	Difficulty concentrating
8:05 p.m.	Increased pulse and heart rate
8:10 p.m.	Pleasant drowsiness similar to .3-milligram dose of hyoscine (scopolamine) hydrobromide without anticholinergic effects, no changes in perception

8:15 p.m.	Dizziness
8:20 p.m.	Lying down with eyes closed, no eidetic images
8:25 p.m.	Relaxation
8:30 p.m.	Hypnagogic state, no dreams
9:55 p.m.	Drowsiness wearing off
10:05 p.m.	Afterglow, euphoria
10:25 p.m.	Baseline, no after effects

Based on the quantitative potency rating scale proposed by the Shulgins, the effects here are rated a Plus Two (++). This self-experiment did not confirm the observations made by Hamilton that the effects of eating agara bark include violent tremor, myosis, and a destructive frenzy.

Agara bark has major visionary effects, but adding ereriba leaves induces certain physiological effects that increase, lengthen, or change the nature of the experience.

About thirty piperidine-type alkaloids have been isolated from the bark, among which are himandrine, himbacine, himbadine, himbosine, and himgravine. There is not a positive test for registering the presence of a psychoactive principle. It is suggested that larger doses of bark may have entheogenic properties.

In particular, himbacine has a low toxicity and an antispasmodic activity. It is known to cause muscarinic receptor (M_2) antagonist activity, but it is unknown whether the psychoactive effects of agara are produced via this muscarinic receptor (M_2) antagonism activity. Himbacine in large doses might also exhibit some M_1 antagonist (atropine-like) activity and produce agitation, excitement, and hallucinations.

GB 18 or Alkaloid J is another *Galbulimima* alkaloid, whose chemical structure has not yet been determined. In animal assays, GB 18 produced CNS depression in mice at 50 mg/kg oral and is reported to have "psychotropic properties" because of its lack of influence on the pain threshold in doses of 5 mg/kg oral. It is hypothesized that GB 18 has visionary effects similar to phencyclidine (PCP). Adventitious consumption of the alkaloid, however, resulted in a bitter taste but no visionary effect as with LSD.[3]

Heimia salicifolia

Considered one of the New World's lesser-known psychoactive plants, *H. salicifolia* is defined by Giacomoni as possessing oneirogenic action. The plant is widespread from southern Mexico to Uruguay, Paraguay, and northern Argentina. It is known in Mexico as *sinicuiche* ("herb of the sun") and in Brazil as *abre o sol* ("open the sun") and *herva da vida* ("herb of life"), a term also identifying other inebriant plant species. It was probably used by the cult of the Aztec god Xochipilli, the "Prince of Flowers," and would have been represented in relief on his statues. Mexican natives believe that this plant has sacred and supernatural powers and that it helps them remember long-past events as if they had happened yesterday. It is also said that *H. salicifolia* use makes the remembrance of prenatal events possible.

In Mexico the lightly faded leaves are macerated in water, and the mixture is fermented in the sun. The beverage causes a light inebriation accompanied by dizziness, torpidity, deafness, somnolent euphoria, darkening and dimensional contraction of the surroundings, altered perception of time and space, estrangement from reality, and auditive hallucinations (in some cases violent ones) with perception of distorted sounds and voices seeming to come from great distances. It is also said that excessive use is harmful, with psychotic phenomena possibly resulting. On the other hand, autoexperimentations carried out by Díaz were negative, with no mental alterations, only a troublesome hypothermia.

In popular medicine the plant is employed in gynocological medicine, against syphilis, as a febrifuge, a diuretic, and an aid to digestion.

The identified alkaloids found in *H. salicifolia* belong to the quinolizidine class and include cryogenine, heimine, lyfoline, lythridine, lythrine, nesodine, and sinine. Among these, cryogenine has the most significant pharmacological action, qualitatively reproducing the effect of the plant extract; cryogenine has a tranquillizing and hypothermic effect and when taken orally at a 310 mg dose was not psychotropic.

Homalomena sp.

Homalomena species are widespread in Asia and South America.

It is suggested that *Homalomena* leaves produce violent derangement followed by slumber with visions. *Homalomena* leaves, stems, and roots are alleged to produce hallucinations when ingested in small amounts.

Natives of the Okapa region of Papua New Guinea employ the leaves of an unidentified species alone or with the leaves and bark of *G. belgraveana* in order to induce visions and dreams. Unidentified *Homalomena* species are used for their reported psychoactive properties by the Awa people in the Eastern Highlands and by the Bimin-Kiskusmin people in the western Sepik Province.

Also in Papua New Guinea, *Homalomena cordata* and *H. versteegii (H. lauterbachii)* are present in magic and sorcery practices ("rain magic" and "love magic," respectively), and another species (called *iva iva*) is a component of an ointment that contains coconut oil. In eastern India, *H. aromatica* was known for its aphrodisiac properties, while in Malay a species is used as a poison arrow ingredient. Many *Homalomena* species are aromatic and the roots are employed in popular medicine, in particular for the treatment of skin afflictions.

A psychonautic bioassay was carried out by Benjamin Thomas with a *Homalomena* species identified as *H. lauterbachii*.[4] The leaves were dried in the shade without the application of heat. It is reported that the dose of *Homalomena* leaves needed to achieve psychoactive effects in Papua New Guinea is "several ereriba leaves." A dose of five dried *Homalomena* leaves was chewed slowly and masticated thoroughly for several minutes. The initial observed effects were an acrid taste, burning sensation in the mouth, and irritation of mucous membranes. This was followed by stomach cramps and abdominal pain. These effects are common with species in the Araceae family and indicate the presence of calcium oxalate. No psychoactive effects were observed in this preliminary human bioassay.

Psychoactive substances have not yet been identified in any of the studied species of *Homalomena*. Chemical studies are lacking. Sesquiter-penoids were isolated from *H. aromatica,* along with linalool, chemically related to terpenes and found in several essential oils. Sesquiterpenes including himbacol have also been isolated from the *Galbulimima* bark of Papua New Guinea. Cyclic alcohols including sesquiterpenic lactones are constituents of the alleged psychoactive plants *Cacalia cordifolia* and *C. decomposita* known as *péyotl* in Mexico. Various sesquiterpenoid compounds of unknown pharmacology were recently isolated from the volatile essential oil of European sweet flag, *Acorus calamus,* a plant with suggested psychoactive properties. Unidentified *Homalomena* sp. from Papua New Guinea known as ereriba may also contain sesquiter-penes and linalool, but there is no pharmacological evidence that lin-alool has any hallucinogenic activity. It is hypothesized that the reported psychoactive properties of *Homalomena* leaves are due to the presence of sesquiterpenoids.

Bioassays of the *Homalomena* leaves are strongly discouraged because of their toxic acrid properties.

Hyoscyamus muticus

The ancient Egyptians knew this species under the name *sakran* ("drunk"). It is cited in different papyri included the *Papyrus Ebers,* the primary source of Egyptian pharmacology created in the twelfth century BCE.

H. muticus was, and still is, used as an inebriant (in relationship with the ancient Egyptian Cult of the Dead) and as medicine against asthma, toothache, seasickness, and cramps. In the *Magical Papyrus* of Leiden it is reported to be a recipe for sleeping for two days. It is com-posed essentially of mandrake *(Mandragora officinarum),* henbane *(H. muticus),* ivy *(Hedera heli),* and wine. It is possible that it may induce prophetic dreams. Today in some circles *H. muticus* is known as "dream plant."

H. muticus presents the highest alkaloidal concentration in its genus. It contains principally hyoscyamine.

Kaempferia galanga

Maraba is the local name for the plant *K. galanga* found in the Highlands of Papua New Guinea. The plant rhizome is known among the Fore
people as "dream man," because it is reported to induce dreams. The
rhizome of this plant is used as a hallucinogen in Papua New Guinea.
Perhaps the earliest written documentation was by Italian naturalist and
explorer Luigi D'Albertis in his book of 1880, *New Guinea: What I Did
and What I Saw*. D'Albertis said that while he was on the south coast of
Papua New Guinea, he was given the roots of an unidentified plant that
the local people chewed for its narcotic and intoxicating properties. The
roots of this plant apparently produced pleasant dreams and visions. The
local people suggested that to properly experience the effects of this plant,
tobacco was smoked after the roots were ingested. The identity of this
plant remains a mystery; it was recently proposed that it corresponds to
K. galanga.

Modern experimentation with *K. galanga* for its alleged hallucinogenic effect was originally stimulated in the 1970s by the popular book
Legal Highs by Adam Gottlieb. The author reports that the rhizome was
chewed and ingested and that the active constituents are unidentified
substances within the volatile oils of the rhizome. There aren't contrain-
dications and the plant has a long history of medicinal use.

In a recent human bioassay, using the *K. galanga* rhizome, Benjamin
Thomas didn't experience any visionary effect. The chronology of the
experience is reported below:

9:27 p.m.	Begin chewing 15 grams of maraba rhizome
9:28 p.m.	Hot, spicy, pungent taste
9:30 p.m.	Lachrymation (tears)
9:32 p.m.	Rhizome swallowed
9:33 p.m.	Gagging due to plant fiber, washed down with a glass of water
9:42 p.m.	First alert, mild CNS stimulation, no changes in perception

9:45 p.m.   Increased heart rate

9:50 p.m.   Dizziness

9:52 p.m.   Sitting down with eyes closed, no eidetic images

10:10 p.m.   Buoyant feelings, similar to 5 gram dose of nutmeg

10:15 p.m.   Euphoria, sense of well-being and elevated mood

11:20 p.m.   Lying down with eyes closed, no perceptual changes

11:35 p.m.   Sleep disturbance and restlessness

11:50 p.m.   Insomnia

Beyond the high content of essential oil in the rhizome of this plant, little is known of the chemistry. The rhizome of *K. galanga* is highly aromatic and contains several essential oils. The constituents include borneol, camphene, carene, ethyl-p-methoxycinnamate, methyl-p-cumaric acid, cinnamic acid, ethyl ester, pentadencane, and cinnamaldehyde.

Borneol is a terpene alcohol that resembles camphor. Camphor is a terpene ketone isolated from the camphor laurel tree, *Cinnamomum camphora*. It was formerly used as a "cerebral excitant." The effects of camphor described by Lewin in *Phantastica* are agreeable warmth and tickling of the skin, general excitation of the nerves, an impulse to move, and an ecstatic mental excitation. Camphor is reported to temporarily disturb the intellectual faculties. Based on the structural (chemical) similarities between borneol and camphor, it is possible that borneol also has cerebral excitant effects and temporarily disturbs the intellectual faculties much like camphor.

Data from clinical studies on the pharmacology of *K. galanga* rhizome extracts indicate toxicity in animals and humans. A pharmacological study of the effects of ethanolic extract using the Hippocratic screening test in animals (rabbits) indicated CNS depression, including decreased motor activity, decreased respiratory rate, loss of screen grip, and analgesia. The chemical compounds ethyl cinnamate, ethyl p-methoxycinnamate, and p-methoxycinnamate are constituents of ethanolic extracts. The chemical ethyl cinnamate has recently been demonstrated in clinical studies to have vaso-relaxant effects on the smooth muscles of the rat aorta.

A pharmacological study by Noro found that extracts of *K. galanga* rhizome produce MAOI activity. The MAOI activity of *K. galanga* extracts was comparable to pharmaceutical drugs formerly used in the treatment of depression: isocarboxazid, phenelzine, and tranylcypromine. These MAOI drugs are associated with a toxic psychokinetic reaction. Agitation and hypomanic behavior may also occur, and on rare occasions hallucinations and confusion are observed. Hallucinations are an adverse reaction of acute toxicity with these MAOI agents. The CNS stimulant activity associated with the in vivo inhibition of MAO produced by extracts of *Kaempferia* rhizome is demonstrated by unauthorized human bioassays: an oral dose of 15 grams of *Kaempferia* rhizome resulted in CNS stimulation followed by elevated mood, restlessness, and insomnia.

Chemical compounds known as cyclohexane diepoxides have been isolated from the related Asian species *Kaempferia rotunda* from Southeast Asia. There is no available data on the human pharmacology of these cyclohexane diepoxides. It is presently unknown if these chemical compounds have psychoactive activity.[5]

The other related Asian species *Alpinia galanga* ("greater galangal") and *A. officinarum* ("lesser galangal") contain 1'-acetoxychavicol acetate, 1'-acetoxyeugenol acetate, cadinene, camphor, eugenol, galangin, and methyl-cinnamate; and cineol, eugenol, galangin, linalool, and methyl-cinnamate, respectively. It is reported that some of these constituents may have psychoactive effects. The species *A. galanga* from Asia is said to have psychoactive properties. The effect of *A. galanga* rhizome is similar to LSD.

Eugenol is the chemical 3-hydroxy-4-methoxyallylbenzene. It is the parent compound of a series of analogues with potential psychoactive properties including methoxyeugenol and methyleugenol isolated from nutmeg *(Myristica fragrans)*. These chemical compounds are the precursors of ring-substituted amphetamine derivatives ("Essential Amphetamines"), a result of in vivo amination.

It is hypothesized that the psychoactivity and hallucinogenic properties of *K. galanga* rhizome are due to either the presence of borneol, MAOI activity, or allylbenzene(s) in the essential oil, which is the precursor of a ring-substituted amphetamine derivative. In particular, it is suggested that hallucinogenic activity might be due to constituents of the essential oils. According to Thomas, larger doses of maraba rhizome may, however, be visionary.

Lycopodium spp.

The genus *Lycopodium* contains a unique class of alkaloids related to quinolizidines. In particular huperzine A and huperzine B are potent inhibitors of acetylcholinesterase enzyme that causes the metabolic destruction of acetylcholine (cholinergics), therefore increasing its levels. This improves learning and the memory functions involved.

The isomer found in nature is (-) huperzine A. It has an acetylcholinesterasic inhibition activity higher than (+) huperzine A and (±) huperzine A, and in this respect it is more potent than physostigmine. Other alkaloids in *Lycopodium* spp. have the same effect as huperzines but they are not equally potent. Traces of nicotine were detected in some species, but the concentration is too low to be pharmacologically active.

Considering the fact that cholinergic compounds seem to be dream inducing due to the increase of acetylcholine levels (a neurotransmitter involved in dream chemistry), it is possible that species of *Lycopodium* containing huperzine A and B could have an oneirogenic property.

Lycopodium squarrosum is a typical species of tropical Africa, Asia, the Pacific, eastern Sepik in Papua New Guinea, and parts of Australia. The Nkopo natives of Madang and Morobe Province in Papua New Guinea rub the plant over the body before going to sleep so that they can meet bush-spirits in their dreams. Bush-spirits (common throughout traditional mythology in Papua New Guinea) provide the subject with a song that has spiritual and healing meanings. Once awakened the person must recite the song until it is learned. This species is psychoactive if smoked, while as decoction the effects are more dramatic and long lasting. What follows is a report of a human bioassay carried out by using a water infusion of dried plant material.

11:00–11:15 a.m.	Half of the decoction was ingested; it had a strong odor of fish.
12:10 p.m.	Subtle effect felt. The other half of the decoction was ingested. The subject noted a loosening of mucus in upper nasal cavity. Over the next hour he reported the perception of a dreamy ambience and a kind of watery pressure in the head. His forehead was hot and he experienced some very mild diarrhea and vomiting as well as nausea in the pit of the stomach.
1:10 p.m.	The subject reported a sensation of tripping in a slow, mild but powerful way.

Following this, the subject ceased noting the chronology of the experience. Nausea and vomiting persisted. The first visual effects were noted. Watching light reflect from curved glass or moving water was enjoyable, the surfaces of objects blurred together; visual effects were also compared to the artwork of M. C. Escher. Then the subject reported the perception of a big, soft force field holding energy within himself and later a slight pain in the right kidney. He found it difficult to pay attention to the psychotropic effects because of the nausea and due to worries that he might have poisoned himself. The effects, including nausea, were still mildly present twelve hours later. In retrospect, the subject compared the experience to that induced by mugwort *(Artemisia vulgaris)* and the delirium of influenza. *L. squarrosum* produces huperzine B, lycopodine, lycodoline, and lucidioline.

L. cernuum is employed in medicine. In Nepal it is used in relation with Vishnu; in Surinam it is employed as a charm. It contains cernuine, nicotine, huperzine B, lycodoline, lucidioline, lycopodine, lyconnotine, annotinine, and lycocernuine.

L. gnidioides is smoked in Madagascar after it has been dried in the shade. It produces inebriation with oneiric hallucinations similar to those of *C. sativa*. It contains anhydrolycodoline, gnidioidine, lucidioline, lycoclavine, lycognidine, gnidine, gnidinine, gnidioidine, and huperzine A.

L. selago was employed as an amulet by the Celtic druids and was gathered in a ritual similar to that employed for mistletoe *(Viscum album).* It seems to have narcotic properties; in particular it induces hypnotic narcosis, total stupor, or coma. Other effects are dizziness, vomiting, and loss of consciousness. The species contains huperzine A, lycodoline, isolycodoline, 12-epi-lycodoline, lycopodine, 6-α-hydroxylycopodine, obscurine, β-hydroxyhuperzine A, and acrifoline.

L. serratum is used in Chinese medicine for memory deficits due to old age, Alzheimer's disease, and myasthenia gravis. In Nepal it is used in relation to Vishnu. It contains huperzine A and B, lycopodine, lycodine, lycodoline, lucidioline, serratine, serratinine, serratanine, and serratinidine.

In North America a *Lycopodium* species is employed to produce a mild hypnotic narcosis.[6] In Papua New Guinea, an unidentified species of *Lycopodium* is used in ritual and magic, while the Gimi people use another species as a medicine.

Mimosa hostilis

Probably identifiable in the *tepescohuitl* ("bronze plant") of the Aztecs, today *M. hostilis* is known as *jurema préta* or *ajucá.* In the past, some ethnic groups in northeastern Brazil prepared a "miraculous" inebriant beverage (known as *vinho de jurema*) from the root bark. The bark was boiled for twenty-four hours and honey was added to counteract the bitter taste. Vinho de jurema was employed in the ajucá ceremony of the Pankarurú, Kakiri, Tusha, and Tulnio Indians. This magical religious use influenced the African American rituals of eastern Brazil.

The jurema cult seems to be very ancient and was rather widespread. It was practiced in the past by a number of now vanished or occidentalized tribes; at present, the cult seems to have disappeared. The ceremony was celebrated before going to war; more recently, participants were priests and warriors who knelt down in order to receive their dose. One of the first descriptions of the rite dates back to 1788. In another testimony of 1843 it is reported that some tribes drank the beverage before spending the night sailing in the depths of sleep. In another report it is written that after having ingested vinho de jurema, sorcerers had fantastic and pleasant dreams.

Vinho de jurema is also a popular remedy with tonic and analgesic properties, used against burns, inflammations and wounds (in Mexico), fatigue, discomforts, and nervous breakdown, or as an aphrodisiac (in Brazil), where the bark of the trunk is employed.

Biochemically, an alkaloid initially named nigerine, then demonstrated identical to DMT, was isolated. It would also be present as β-carboline. The effect of vinho de jurema could be explained by the concomitant presence of DMT and β-carboline or by the concomitant ingestion of an additive containing MAOI compounds.

Myristica fragrans

Nutmeg is a spice but also a medicinal and magical plant. In the ayurvedic medicine of ancient India it was known as *mada shaunda* ("narcotic fruit"). In India it is added to tobacco and then chewed or snuffed. The natives of Indonesia also snuffed nutmeg and added it to betel (the nut of the palm *Areca catechu*). The Egyptians use it as a marijuana substitute, and the natives of Malaysia believe that it drives demons out of the possessed. *Myristica fragrans* is cited as a component of a magical perfume in *The Key of Solomon the King* by Clavicula Salomonis. Medicinally, it is used for digestive problems, asthma, and heart complaints.

The intoxicating properties of nutmeg are well known. Intoxication, when it happens, often occurs accidentally rather than intentionally. Nutmeg is sometimes used as a substitute for other unavailable or unaffordable substances, and it can be defined as a pseudo hallucinogen. It can be eaten, smoked, or snuffed as a marijuana substitute.

Nutmeg is an inebriant and sedative, induces sleep and delirium, and is also an aphrodisiac. The experience is characterized by unpleasant side effects (headache, dizziness, nausea, stomach cramps, and tachycardia), time and space distortion, detachment from reality, sensation of flying or floating, and a feeling of having the limbs separated from the body.

In a self-experiment Paul Devereux ingested two level teaspoons of ground nutmeg, also sprinkling the essential oil on pillows and sheets before going to sleep. He suffered mild nausea and irritation of the skin. He had a conscious dream in which he was traveling through a tunnel, flying at ever increasing speed.

In general it seems that nutmeg-induced dreams are more intense and colorful. In other cases nutmeg caused "changes" in dreams, bizarre dreams, and also lucid ones. One subject reported that after ingesting nutmeg and then going to sleep, his bedroom became changed and there was a dark figure lying next to him in the bed. In that moment he realized he was dreaming. In this case the lucidity could have been the consequence of the nightmare episode.[7]

Nutmeg contains an essential oil composed of safrole, eugenol, iso-eugenol, myristicin α-and β-pinene, α-phellandrene, and limonene. Myristicin and safrole have a stimulating and, in high doses, toxic effect. They are probably aminated in the human body, producing 3-methoxy-4, 5-methylenedioxyamphetamine (MMDA), and 3, 4-methylenedioxyamphetamine (MDA), respectively.

Salvia divinorum

S. divinorum is an endemic plant of the Mazatec region of Oaxaca, Mexico, probably not native to the area. It was known to the Aztecs as *pipilzintzintli* ("the noblest little prince"), and today it is called *la hembra* ("the female"), *hierba María* ("herb of Mary"), and *hojas de la pastora* or *ska pastora* ("leaves of the shepherdess").

Its use as a shamanic inebriant is reported only in the Mazatec region. The first modern witness in this regard dates back to 1939 when Jean B. Johnson observed the use of *S. divinorum* by a shaman in the context of the ingestion of psilocybian mushrooms (essentially, *Psilocybe* spp.) and seeds of *Convolvulaceae* for divination. In 1961 Robert Gordon Wasson became the first nonnative known to experiment with the effects of the plant. He described the ingestion of the leaves after mastication as well as the preparation of a water infusion of the same leaves followed by manual squeezing. Wasson compared the effect to that of psilocybian mushrooms, but said it was less ample and lasting. It seems that the full effects are best perceived in darkness and silence while slowly breathing and remaining still. Duration varies according to the ingestion technique.

Generally the effects can be described as follows: sensation of movements, perception of voices or inner murmurs, bidimensional surfaces, bizarre geometries, simultaneous realities, visits to places in the past, contacts with "entities," sensation of being transformed into objects, loss of bodily and personal identity, and out of body experiences.

On the basis of personal experimentations, in 1975 Díaz classified the plant as an oneirogen, a classification reconsidered in more recent studies. *S. divinorum* is an oneirogen (and not a true hallucinogen) because it would induce REM activity episodes during wakefulness, leading to involuntary experiences of preconscious or conscious dream. According to some scholars, the fact that the plant's effects stand out best in darkness and silence while the subject breathes slowly and remains still, qualifies it as a good preparation for the mind before consciously entering the oneiric world.

In Mazatec popular medicine, *S. divinorum* has a topical use; for example, the infusion is employed for a bath or the residue of the leaf extract is applied on the patient's head as a poultice. Other uses are as a stimulant and tonic, for digestive problems, and against headache, rheumatisms, and magical disease.

The active principle of *S. divinorum* is recognized as diterpene salvinorin A. The most potent effect is obtained with sublingual administration of the pure compound. The leaves are more active if chewed and maintained in the mouth rather than ingested. Infusion is the least effective technique of administration. The dried and smoked leaves are active.

Scirpus sp.

The Tarahumara Indians of Mexico called a species of *Scirpus* (probably *Scirpus atrovirens*) *bakana* (or *bakanawa*), corresponding to the name of the psychoactive cactus *Coryphantha compacta*.

This plant grows in Chihuahua and is one of the most important psychoactive plants known by the Tarahumara. It is a potent narcotic with a rather widespread local use and is used particularly as a substitute for peyote.

The Indians have great respect for this plant, and they even fear cultivating it. They believe that if the plant is mutilated it is capable of emitting high noises that lead to insanity and that the responsible person could die or go permanently mad. Before its use, one has to take the precaution of dedicating chants or offering food. The bulbs are collected during special expeditions (or obtained during exchanges) and are employed as an agent for divination, and in order to dream during the night. It is said that after having eaten the bulbs the person falls into a deep sleep during which he undertakes long travels and speaks with long-dead relatives; there are also brilliant and colorful visions. As for other uses, healers employ it as a protective amulet against physical and mental illnesses, for curing those illnesses, and also against pain. The bulbs are also worn on the body to counteract madness.

Specific biochemical data are not available. However, in the genus and species of *Cyperus* (of the same family to which the species belongs), as well as in other related genera, β-carbolines of the harmala type and other alkaloids were isolated. On the other hand, there is evidence that some species of *Cyperus* could be infested by parasitic mushrooms producing ergot alkaloids, possibly psychoactive.

Silene capensis

The available ethnobotanical data for *S. capensis* are reported by Manton Hirst and deal with the diviners *(amagqirha)* of the Xhosa people living in the eastern Cape of South Africa. Here the plant is considered a medicinal root *(ubulawu)* under the name of *undlela ziimhlophe,* translated as "white ways" or "white paths." The root is a gift *(usipho)* of the ancestors and is part of the offerings in the initiation rites of the diviners.

The most important use of this powdered root is as an oneirogen in the training of female novice diviners and healers. The main effect is the production of lucid and even prophetic dreams, reported by the novices to their initiation diviners. There are two kinds of dream experience reported; the first is characterized by symbolic elements and deals with the dreamer's issues, while the other is more distinctly prophetic, in immediate and direct relation to elements of the dreamer's life, which will be manifested in the future. All varieties of ubulawu produce lucid dreams. They differ in the dream imagery they produce according to the location of growing; for example, those growing near a river, in grassland, or in a forest will induce dreams associated with the river, the grassland, or the forest, respectively.

The ingestion of the root is the only genuine way in which to establish whether a person is truly called by the ancestors to become a diviner. Only the chosen one will dream, while ordinary people can ingest the root even in great quantity without having any dreams. Only Xhosa diviners can identify, pick, and use the plant. The place of picking is shown to the diviner in a dream, during which the whole plant is surrounded by white light. The next morning, the diviner will go to the place he saw in the dream and pick the plant.

S. capensis is used as an emetic medicine and also to cure madness. The crushed root is put in water and given to the mad person to drink. Eventually he will become calm and start talking.

Hirst reports some experimental data on the use of *S. capensis:* During an afternoon, after a day of fasting, he ingested some 200–250 mg of powdered root in water. The taste was faintly bitter, but apart from this, there were not other physical side effects. After about twenty minutes he saw wavy lines of light in front of him, like luminous reflections on the surface of the moving water of a river; the experiment terminated one hour later. In the early hours of the next morning, he suddenly awoke, trembling and panting. He had experienced the most vivid dream of his life, a dream with a mythical content and a prophetic meaning, clearly remembered even twenty-five years later. He never reported alterations in his ordinary waking consciousness.

In another experiment, a professor of pharmacy at the University of Rhodes, after chewing a small piece of *S. capensis,* experienced mild effects with perception of abstract shapes and colors.

In the 1970s two postgraduate psychology students ingested large quantities of the root obtained from a Xhosa diviner, but after various attempts they didn't succeed in dreaming.

Recently Gianluca Toro carried out bioassays by ingesting the pulverized root of the plant in different weighed quantities, in the afternoon or immediately before sleeping. The results are reported below.

Taking 100 mg in the afternoon, the first effects came fifteen to twenty minutes later. Shadows appeared at the edges of the visual field, followed by phosphenes (brilliant points rapidly emerging from the sky). Then something like a slowly vanishing azure mist was perceived in the distance. The total duration was approximately one hour and during the night there were no remarkable dreams.

With the ingestion of 60 mg before sleeping, after thirty minutes, there were some vague brilliant points and luminous straight lines. During the first stage of sleep, the mental imagery seemed a little more intense than usual, with perception of geometric patterns, some of them colored or in motion. No particular dream was remembered the next morning.

Thirty minutes after ingesting 200 mg before sleep, some discrete undulating luminous lines and vague shadows were perceived, along with some small variations in the intensity of reflected light. There was a slight improvement of mental imagery (perception of unusual forms and reticules), but no significant dreams.

It seems that the root can be considered a very mild psychedelic, without physical side effects. The fact that several experiments failed to produce any remarkable dreams (merely a slight increase in the production of hypnagogic imagery) could be related to the particular cultural and emotional context of the experimenters.

Until now *S. capensis* has not been widely known, and the available pharmacological data is scarce. Members of the family to which *S. capensis* belongs produce anthocyanins, pinitol, and triterpenoid saponins. The active principle(s) of *S. capensis* could be hypothetically represented by some triterpenoid saponin. However, in preliminary chemical analyses by Thin Layer Chromatography (TLC), no known "entheogenically" relevant compounds were found.[8]

Turbina corymbosa

This plant was very important among the ancient Aztecs, Zapotecs, and Maya, and it is still used in modern times. Called *coaxihuitl* ("snake plant"), its seeds were named *ololiuhqui* ("round things") and were consumed in water infusion.

According to chroniclers of the Spanish Conquest period, the plant was used as a medicine against many health problems and to contact the spirits of the dead. When the priests employed the seeds for this purpose they became senseless and saw devilish forms and phantoms. The seeds of ololiuhqui are also used for divination purposes. The Aztec priests believed that the seeds contained a spirit that would manifest itself after ingestion, answering questions especially about the future. The seeds were also used as an aphrodisiac.

The Maya use the seeds for divination and for medicinal purposes. They call the plant *xtabentum* ("precious stone cord"), and it is taken in order to find lost or stolen objects and to recognize a thief. Before the user falls asleep, others speak into his ear, asking, "Where is the lost object?" During sleep the person sees where the object can be found.

The seeds contain ergot alkaloids such as lysergic acid amide, chanoclavine, elymoclavine, and lysergol.

Ugni candollei

Recently C. Aldunate del Solar reviewed the visionary plants employed by the Mapuche of Chile. The Mapuche classify visionary medicinal plants *(perrimontuelawen)* in three categories:

- "bad" or "strong" medicines *(weishawelawen)*
- medicines acting through dreams *(pewmawelawen)*
- medicines against evil encounters *(trafunmawelawen)*

The pewmawelawen plants cure through dreams and are used to communicate with ancestors, to submit questions on the future, and to get news about people who are located far away. Ancient warrior leaders probably employed these plants to prepare themselves for battle, and sorcerers used them to spy upon their victims. In this class we find *U. candollei (ugni)*, *Pellaea ternifolia (piukelawen)*, and other unidentified species known as *fushkulawen* ("fresh medicinal plants") and *kotrokachu* ("salty herb").

U. candollei is widespread along parts of the coast of Chile. One species found on the shores of Valdivia is considered a particularly potent species, used for inducing dreams in combination with plants such as *P. ternifolia* and other nonspecified pewmawelawen. *Pellaea cordata*, known in Mexico as *itamo real*, has inebriant properties. In Chile the fruits of *U. candollei*, known as trautrau (see *D. spinosa*) are employed as additives to *chicha*, a fermented beverage prepared with maize and commonly used in Central and South America.

The medicinal use of *U. candollei* is scarcely known. The term *fushkulawen* is reported on the coast of Valdivia and could be a generic name for refreshing plants that cure diseases caused by heat.

No phytochemical data are available.

Xeromphis sp.

Data about this plant have been reported by Christian Rätsch.

In Nepal, the inhalation of smoke produced by the burning of the flowers of the *maidal* plant induces somnolence and a quiet dream-filled sleep. Alternatively, the fruits are pounded and put in a cup that is placed over burning coals before going to sleep. In some cases the pounded fruits are combined with other plants for inhalation, such as *Juniperus recurva*, *Rhododendron anthopogon*, *R. lepidotum*, or the resin of *Shorea robusta*. It is also possible to smoke the fruits along with tobacco *(N. tabacum)* to produce a stronger effect. A mixture of fruits of maidal, tobacco, angel's trumpet *(D. metel)*, and hemp *(C. sativa)* can be prepared by triturating the components in equal parts and making them into a cigarette. The mixture can be strewn on embers and the smoke inhaled. The external involucre of the fruits is resinous and can be smoked.

Until now, botanical identification of this plant has been uncertain. Probably it is *Xeromphis spinosa* whose Nepalese name is *maidal,* (sacred to Shiva in India). Alternative attributions are *Randia dumetorum* (the fruits have an irritant and emetic action and are employed as fish poison), *X. uliginosa,* and, less probably, *Litsea sebifera* or *L. glutinosa,* the latter with antibacterial, antimycotic, and aphrodisiac properties.

In popular medicine, *X. spinosa* is used as an emetic, against amoebic dysentery, malaria, and as fish poison.

No biochemical data are available.

Minor Oneirogenic Plant Species

In this section we briefly explore some other minor plant species to which oneirogenic properties are attributed.

Acorus calamus

The roots of *A. calamus* are combined with *V. officinalis* roots to prepare a tea, which enhances lucid dreaming.[9] It contains α- and β-asarone, acorine, neoacorone, curcumene, humulene, caryophyllene, and decadienale.

Artemisia absinthium

A. absinthium is used to prepare the liqueur with the same name, possibly stimulating dreams defined as "strange" according to a report.[10] It principally contains thujone.

Borago officinalis

In 1725 the physician Valentin Kräutermann reports in *Der Curieuse und vernünfftige Zauber-Arzt* (The Curious and Wise Enchanter Doctor) that borage can induce dreams. *B. officinalis* contains kaempferol, bornesitol, and choline.[11]

Cannabis sativa

Hemp is one of the oldest cultivated plants in human history, largely employed as raw material, medicine, inebriant, and aphrodisiac. It is cited in the ancient Greek and Latin literature, and it is believed that Celtic druids knew its psychoactive properties. Among the ancient Germans it was sacred to the love goddess Freya.

In ancient China it was considered as a divine plant, and the Taoists ate it in order to increase their concentration while reading the sacred texts. Hemp is found in Chinese herbals and medical texts, where it is reported that if taken in excess one can see devils and spirits. The Taoist alchemists burned incense made from hemp flowers in order to have visions and reach immortality. In tantric rituals hemp induced erotic ecstasy; in the yogic system it would sustain the spiritual powers, while Sufis reached religious ecstasy by using this plant.

In many parts of the world hemp is normally combined with other psychoactive substances (above all in smoking mixtures, opium, thornapple, and tobacco). Hemp intensifies oneiric production. It contains Δ^9-THC.

Curcuma longa

C. longa is a mild aromatic stimulant. In some cases REM periods, dream imagery, vividness, and dream recall can be greatly increased by this plant.[12] It contains α-phellandrene, sabinene, cineol, pinene, bisabolene, borneol, camphor, caryophyllene, limonene, linalool, and eugenol.

Epilobium angustifolium

The flowers of *E. angustifolium*, when smoked, enhance lucid dreaming, producing a subtle but definite effect. The plant is used by Siberian shamans in combination with *Amanita muscaria*. American Indians used a poultice of *E. angustifolium* to treat burns and skin sores.[13] The phytochemical data are unknown.

Ginkgo biloba

Ginkgo is used in limited cases to treat tinnitus. It has displayed dream-altering properties and the ability to improve dream recall.[14] It contains diterpenes, sesquiterpenes, and pinitol.

Ilex guayusa

I. guayusa could induce brief dreams to forsee whether a hunting expedition will be fruitful according to the Jibaro of Amazonia. It is reported that the plant can also induce lucid dreams. It is an ayahuasca additive meant to mitigate the bitter taste of the beverage, inspire strength during its drinking, and prevent malaises. In Ecuadorian Amazonia, a tea made with *I. guayusa* is employed in ritual purifications, as an aphrodisiac, and as a tonic for the treatment of headache and stomach problems. The leaves contain a significant quantity of caffeine, as well as triterpenes.

Melissa officinalis

In 1547 the erudite G. Cardano discussed in *De subtilitate rerum* the effect of certain plants on sleep and dreams. He wrote that the balm mint (probably *Melissa officinalis*) caused pleasant and agreeable dreams. This fact was confirmed by Kräutermann in *Der Curieuse und vernünfftige Zauber-Arzt*. *M. officinalis* contains sesquiterpenes, α- and β-citrale, citronellal, citronellol, linalool, geraniol, isogeraniol, thymol, and ethyl benzoate.

Mellitis melissophyllum

Giam Battista Della Porta in *Magia naturalis* (1588) reports that an excessive search for sensations has led witches to abuse certain natural substances. After dinner, before going to sleep, if the witches chew *hypoglossa, melysophyllon,* or some similar plants, they will have beautiful and cheerful dreams. They will see plants, meadows, trees, flowers, and luxuriant green lands covered with beautiful shadows.[15] *Melysophyllon* could be *M. melissophyllum*. It contains caryophyllene, citronellol, citronellal, geranial, geraniol, and nereal.

Opium Substitutes

Several plants used in various forms (entire plant, leaves, seeds, latex, tincture) can serve as opium substitutes. These plants are *Aesculus californicus* and *A. pavia* (aesculin); *Argemone mexicana* and *A. platyceras* (*chicalote*; contains principally berberine and protropine); *Bernoullia flammea (amapola blanca); D. hopwoodii* (contains nicotine and nornicotine); *Eschscholzia californica* (*amapola amarilla*; contains magnoflorine, norargemonine, *bis*-norargemonine, and protropine); *Euphorbia* spp.; *Lactuca virosa, L. sativa, L. serriola,* and *L. quercina* (*lactucarium*; contains lactucine and lactucopicrine); *Monotropa uniflora; Mitragyna speciosa* (*kratom*; contains mitragynine); *Papaver bracteatum* (contains thebaine); and *Papaver rhoeas* (contains berberine, rhoeadine, and protropine).

Papaver somniferum

P. somniferum is the source of opium that can stimulate dream production. It contains morphine, codeine, papaverine, and narcotine.

Piper methysticum

The roots of *P. methysticum* are traditionally employed in Oceania in the preparation of a beverage known as *kava-kava,* which is used in ceremonial and religious contexts and as an offering to the gods and ancestors. The effect is muscular relaxation and a kind of quiet alcoholic euphoria (maybe achieving psychedelic action in high doses) with the possibility of inducing vivid and lucid dreams.[16] In combination with valerian root, one subject experienced very interesting dreams that were much longer and clearer than normal. The subject remembered the dreams very well after waking and for several days afterward. The plant also finds its use in ethnogynaecology against venereal diseases, as an antiseptic, and for soothing inflammations and bites. The active principles include yangonine, methysticin, and dihydromethysticin.

Polypodium vulgare

In the previously cited work *Der Curieuse und vernünfftige Zauber-Arzt,* Kräutermann reported that polypody can induce dreams. *P. vulgare* contains saponines, polypodine (a physiological inactive glycoside), a phytosterine, and benzoic acid.

Potentilla reptans

In the past the creeping cinquefoil, *Potentilla reptans* (a plant with magical powers, according to the ancients), had a reputation as an oneirogenic species. It contains catecutanic acid and tormentilline.

Rhodiola rosea

R. rosea is a plant employed in Scandinavian and Russian traditional medicine with numerous applications. It is an adaptogen, has stimulant properties, and counteracts pain, mental exhaustion, and physical fatigue. *R. rosea* increases physical strength and resistance; cures scurvy, altitude sickness, headache, infections, inflammations, depression, hysteria, disorders of the nervous system; and increases longevity. In Central Asia it is used against colds and influenza; in Mongolia it is prescribed for tuberculosis and cancer. It is reported that the plant could interfere with sleep or cause vivid dreams. Among the classes of compounds isolated from this species we cite the phenylpropanoids (rosavine, rosine, and rosarine), phenylethanol derivatives (salidroside and tirosol), and monoterpenes (rosiridol and rosaridine). It is supposed that other species of *Rhodiola* have similar oneirogenic properties.

Ruscus hypoglossum

The *Ruscus* species could be identified with *hypoglossa,* cited by Della Porta in *Magia naturalis* (see *Mellitis melissophyllum*). *Hypoglossa* is also cited by Pliny the Elder in *Historia Naturalis* and could be identified with *R. hypoglossum*. Phytochemical data haven't been found.

Salvia sp.

A not yet identified species of *Salvia* is employed as an oneirogen in Mexico by the Nahuatl Indians of Sierra de Puebla, where it is known as *xiwit*. The phytochemical data are not available.

Souroubea spp.

Souroubea crassipetala and *Souroubea guianensis* are species known in Colombian Amazonia as "witches' narcotic." According to our knowledge, no phytochemical data are available.

Tabernanthe iboga

Used principally in the Bwiti cult of Gabon, initiates take massive quantities of the powdered root of *T. iboga*. At low doses the plant is a stimulant and aphrodisiac, while at higher doses it is visionary and permits contact with the world of the ancestors and spirits. After the ingestion of ibogaine (the major active component of the plant), there is skin torpidity and auditive buzzing accompanied by an oscillating sound and the perception of an intense vibration of objects. Phenomena are frequently observed in conscious dreaming. In practice, ibogaine induces a "waking dream" state. The species principally contains ibogaine, ibogamine, tabernanthine, and voacangine.

Valeriana officinalis

The roots of *V. officinalis* are combined with *A. calamus* roots to prepare a tea, which promotes lucid dreaming.[17] It contains camphene, pinene, limonene, borneol, valerianone, valerianic acid, and bornil isovalerianate.

Vanilla planifolia

An orchid known by the ancient Aztecs as *tlilxochitl*, *V. planifolia* was used as an additive to chocolate and to *balché,* a fermented and sacred beverage derived from honey. This drink was typical of the prehispanic Maya, Yucatecs, and Lacandons. *V. planifolia* is also added to tobacco-containing preparations and is employed in love magic. It seems also that its fragrance induces sweet dreams. The plant contains vanillin (with a chemical structure similar to that of male pheromones), coumarin, and essential oils. Alkaloids are generally uncommon in orchids.

Verbena officinalis

V. officinalis (vervain) was an important magical plant. It was the *hiera-botane* ("sacred plant") of the ancients. Vervain was a plant sacred to the Celts (who called it "druid's weed") and was used by the druids in magical preparations and cures. The Romans used the plant (known as *verbenaca* or *Veneris herba,* "herb of Venus") in love rituals. According to Pliny the plant had to be picked using a particular rite. He also reported that the druids employed vervain in divination practices. If rubbed on the skin, a person could obtain anything he or she desired; it heals all diseases and facilitates friendship. During medieval times, vervain was considered a plant with great magical power. It was supposed to give strength, refresh the mind, and cure all diseases. It was also used as an amulet against demons, ghosts, evil spirits, evil eyes, and temptations of witches.

Vervain was purported to have aphrodisiac properties and to induce wondrous prophetic dreams. European witches probably employed it in enchantments and curses and in the making of ointments. It is found in an "astrological recipe" reported by Johann Hartlieb in his *Das Buch aller verbotenen Künste* (1456).[18] This ointment was employed for flying. It is also possible that vervain had a depurative action against the more toxic components of the ointment itself.

In modern times no psychoactive action has been recognized for vervain. The plant contains glycosides such as verberine and verbenalin (causing sedation and slowing the heartbeat), hastatoside, and essential oils. In some experiments with animals, motor excitation and convulsions were observed. However, the pharmacology is not clear.

In respect to all the plants known and used by man for psychoactive purposes, the oneirogenic ones aren't numerous, but their use has a significative value. The prototypic and most known oneirogenic plant is *C. zacatechichi,* the only species scientifically tested on humans in order to evaluate its dream-inducing properties. Other species whose properties are especially worth studying are those employed in traditional ritual contexts, such as *G. belgraveana, K. galanga, L. squarrosum, S. divinorum, S. capensis,* and *T. iboga.*

5

Oneiromagicals

Oneirogens in Ancient and Modern Magic

Magic could be intended as a way to modify the world in order to follow a precise purpose, a secret knowledge. Every human culture in the world performed (and performs) magic actions by means of proper rituals and tools; magic is activated by rituals and directed by tools. Plants are one of the most important tools. They can be plants of prophecy, magical medicines, and ingredients in elixirs of immortality, aphrodisiacs, poisons, and death charms. They are used in mysteries, libations, ritual circles, vision quests, incantations, oracles, sacrifices, hunting magic, and eroticism. The anthropological research has demonstrated that magical plants are generally psychoactive.

This chapter deals with a selection of plants and preparations used in the context of magical beliefs, in ancient and modern times, comprising species to which somewhat controlled references and more or less reliable witnesses attribute oneirogenic properties.[1]

These plants are employed in ointments, pills, infusions, burners, or as "dream pillows." A dream pillow is stuffed with aromatic herbs and then tucked under the head; as a sleeping person tosses and turns restlessly, the herbs are crushed to exude their scent.

Kyphi

Surely the most renowned and legendary perfume produced in ancient Egypt was kyphi. Its use can be traced back at least to the sixteenth century BCE in a ceremonial religious context under the control of praying priests.

There were many preparations of kyphi, and the number of ingredients was variable. The original recipe is reproduced on the walls of the Egyptian temple of Edfu (third to first century BCE) consecrated to the god Horus. Another recipe is reported in the *Papyrus Ebers*. Maneton, an Egyptian priest and writer of the third century BCE, wrote a book titled *About the Preparation of Kyphis*. It is believed that Plutarch (first century CE) derived the ingredients from Maneton and presented the recipe in *De Iside et Osiride*. A recipe for kyphi is also reported by Dioscorides (first century CE) in his *Materia Medica*.

Kyphi was induced via fumigation, ingestion, and perhaps as an ointment. It had many uses. It could create a dreamy state of happiness, aid communication with the gods, and uplift the spirit. Plutarch states that under the influence of kyphi the body has a propitious disposition to sleep. The perfume purifies the imaginative and oneiric faculty. Kyphi also had medicinal properties; it was used in curing lung diseases, asthma, liver disorders, for the purification of intestines, and other ailments.

A list of ingredients found in one kyphi recipe includes aspalathos, bitumen, cardamom, cinnamon, cyperus, fenugreek, frankincense, honey, juniper, lentisk, mastic, mint, myrrh, olibanum, pistacia resin, raisins, rumex, rush, seseli, thornapple, styrax juice, sweet flag, and wine.

Rush is the translation of the Greek term *thryon* and refers to plants of the genus *Juncus*. These plants can sometimes be infested by parasitic mushrooms of the Clavicipitaceae family producing ergot alkaloids. Among species of *Juncus*, Dioscorides reports one called *eyripike schoinos*. Its seeds induce sleep and also lethargy. Pliny reports two species of *Juncus* called *holoschoenus* and *euripicen*. *Holoschoenus* causes headaches, and *euripicen* induces sleep and lethargy if used in excessive doses. *Thryon* also corresponds to *strychnos,* which refers to thornapple *(Datura stramonium).*

Cyperus corresponds to the genus *Cyperus.* Perhaps the species employed was *Cyperus rotundus.* Pliny identified the following species of *Cyperus: Cyperus esculentus, C. papyrus,* and *C. rotundus. C. esculentus* along with *C. rotundus* are reported as *cyperon,* which, when taken as a potion, provokes dilatation of the uterus and when used in excess causes uterine expulsion. The ash of *C. papyrus (papyrum),* when taken in wine, is sleep inducing. Species of *Cyperus* could be infested by *Balansia cyperi,* a parasitic mushroom producing ergot alkaloids like ergobalansine and ergobalansinine.

Sweet flag is identified with *A. calamus.* The oil of the rhizome is a tonic and stimulant, while the free alcoholic extract of the essential oil has sedative and analgesic effects. It contains α- and β-asarone that seem to possess hypnotic properties. At high doses sweet flag produces an effect similar to that of LSD, and an aqueous decoction of the powdered root can provoke a moderate psychedelic and visionary experience lasting several hours.

The term *styrax* could refer to *Styrax officinalis, S. benzoin,* or *Liquidambar* spp. *S. officinalis* contains the resinous substances cinnameine and vanillin. *S. benzoin* can be lightly psychoactive. It possesses a balsamic scent and contains benzoic, cinnamic, and siaresinolic acid; coniferilbenzoate; vanillin; styrol; and benzaldehyde. Some species of *Liquidambar* have shown the presence of styrol, vanillin, styrocamphene, cinnamic acid, and acetyl cinnamate.

Cinnamon *(Cinnamomum verum)* is a plant with tonic and stimulant properties as well as aphrodisiac ones. It is said that, when cinnamon is smoked, it has a cannabis-like effect. It contains cinnamaldehyde, benzaldehyde, furfurol, caryophyllene, phellandrene, pinene, cymol, and eugenol. Cassia *(Cinnamomum cassia)* was used in Egypt as a liturgic fumigation. The bark contains cinnamaldehyde, cinnamyl acetate, phenylpropyl acetate, cinncassiol A, cinnzeilanol, cinnzeilanine, benzaldehyde, and coumarin.

The term *olibanum* refers to species of the genus *Boswellia* containing pinene, limonene, candinene, camphene, cymene, borneol, verbenon, verbenol, dipentene, phellandrene, and olibanol.

Frankincense can be identified with *Boswellia thurifera;* it played an important role in the Egyptian religious cult. It was sacred to Ammon and was also used by Egyptian magicians to invoke demons. Frankincense possesses a stimulant property.

Myrrh *(Commiphora molmol)* was known as "tears of Horus." It was sacred to Hathor, the goddess of inebriation, and ritually employed. According to Dioscorides, *Commiphora myrrha* induces sleep and is good for frenetics when used as a saffron ointment on the head. Myrrh contains pinene, limonene, cinnamic and cuminic aldehyde, cresol, mirrolic acid, and eugenol.

Juniper might be identified with *Juniperus communis.* The active principles are concentrated mostly in the berries. They include α-pinene, sabinene, camphene, candinene, juniperol, juniperine, junene, and terpineol-4. Another identification for juniper might be *Juniperus macrocarpa.*

Lentisk (pistacia resin, mastic) *(Pistacia lentiscus)* contains α-and β-masticoresene, masticinic, masticolic and masticonic acid, and α-pinene.

Rumex (probably *Rumex obtusifolius*) has tonic properties, and cardamom *(Elettaria cardamomum)* is rich in essential oils.

Another component of kyphi was galbanum *(Ferula* spp., especially *Ferula galbaniflua)* whose resinous exudate has a heavy aroma. It has stimulant and fixative properties and contains galbaresenic and galbanic acid, candinene, pinene, and umbelliferone.

Ointments and Pills

A particular class of flowering plants is represented by the psychoactive *Solanaceae.* In the past this class of plants, informally known as the nightshade family, was combined with certain other plants and reported in magical recipes and used especially in ointments

The psychoactive *Solanaceae* are very toxic plant species. Their use is extremely dangerous, in some cases leading to very serious harm and death. The active compounds responsible for the action are the tropane alkaloids atropine, hyoscyamine, and scopolamine. In general they cause psychic and motor excitation, dimming of consciousness, clumsiness, visual and auditive hallucinations, and intense and violent delirium. Other effects are fatigue, somnolence and torpor, deep sleep with nightmares, even coma and death due to respiratory failure in cases of excessive doses.

In *The Secretes of the Reverende Master Alexis of Piedmont*, written in 1559, the author Alexis lists some plants that induce marvelous dreams. Eating solanum or mandrake at night, or the herb apollinaris, makes one see beautiful and graceful things during sleep.[2]

Solanum corresponds to a species of the *Solanaceae* family (probably *Atropa belladonna, Solanum nigrum,* or *S. dulcamara*). Mandrake is identified with *Mandragora officinarum* (or *M. autumnalis*), while the herb *apollinaris* (henbane) can be represented by *Hyoscyamus* sp. *(H. niger).* All these plants are psychoactive.

The physician Johann Wier, in *De praestigiis daemonum* (1563), lists the ingredients of three magical ointments useful in procuring long dreams. The first contains hemlock *(Cicuta virosa* or *Conium maculatum),* juice of aconite *(Aconitum napellus),* poplar leaves *(Populus* sp., *Populus nigra),* and soot. The second ointment contains hemlock, iris *(Iris pseudacorus),* creeping cinquefoil (Potentilla sp., *Potentilla reptans),* blood of a bat, deadly nightshade *(Atropa belladonna),* and oil. The third is prepared with fat of a recently born baby, juice of hemlock, aconite, creeping cinquefoil, deadly nightshade, and soot. The active ingredients are deadly nightshade and possibly aconite and hemlock.

We must point out that the mention of using the fat of a baby was for the purpose of inducing fear and repugnance, and it is not an acceptable practice today.

In the work *De la lycanthropie, transformation et extase des sorcièrs (On Lycanthropy, Transformation and Ecstasy of Sorcerers)* (1615) by the physician Jean de Nynauld, there is a recipe for a dream-inducing ointment that supposedly allowed witches to attend the Sabbath in a dream state. In the composition we find the fat of reptiles, parsley (probably not the plant commonly known with this name, *Petroselium crispum,* but a species of hemlock to which it is very similar), aconite, creeping cinquefoil, black nightshade *(S. nigrum),* and caterpillars. The active ingredients are black nightshade, aconite, and hemlock.

Pierre V. Piobb reports some interesting recipes in his *Formulaire de Haute-Magie* written in the nineteenth century.

> "Dream pills." Rind of cynoglossa root *(Cynoglossum officinale),* seeds of henbane *(Hyoscyamus niger),* opium extract *(P. somniferum),* myrrh *(Balsamodendron myrrha),* olibanum *(Boswellia spp.),* saffron *(Crocus sativus),* castor, and opium syrup.

According to the author, the ingestion of one or two pills before going to bed would give a pleasant sleep with sweet dreams. The effect would be due principally to henbane and opium.

> "Infernal ointment." Human fat, hashish, hemp flowers (*Cannabis* sp.), common poppy flowers *(P. rhoeas),* powdered hellebore root *(Helleborus niger),* and grains of sunflower *(Helianthus annuus).* The ingredients are put in a container with hemp and poppy flowers. The container is closed and warmed in a water bath for two hours and then the material is filtered.

According to the author, before going to sleep the preparation is smeared behind the ears, on the neck (carotid), the armpits, the area of the sympathetic nerve, the soles, wrists, and the fold of the arms. During sleep it induces the sensation of being at the Sabbath. The effect would be principally due to hemp.

Perhaps one of the most important modern experimenters with witches' ointment was Karl Kiesewetter, a German erudite and occultist who at the end of the 1800s undertook some tests. He smeared his body with an ointment prepared following a recipe of Della Porta and reported in *Magia naturalis.* This ointment was composed with the fat of a child, *eleoselinum* (celery, *Apium graveolens),* aconite, poplar branches, and soot, or with *sium (Sium erectum, S. sisarum,* or *Rorippa sylvestris),* common acorus *(I. pseudacorus* or *A. calamus),* creeping cinquefoil, blood of a bat, solanum, and oil. He had the impression of flying through a tornado. He fell into a long sleep and the following night had very intense dreams with fast trains and marvelous tropical landscapes. He dreamed of being on a mountain and speaking to the people in the valley below.[3] He also wrote of having dreams of flying in colored spirals. The active ingredients are solanum and possibly aconite.

In 1960 Will-Erich Peuckert, an ethnology professor at the University of Göttingen, experimented with an ointment prepared according to a seventeenth-century recipe and essentially composed of fat, wild celery (perhaps a wild variety of *A. graveolens),* parsley, deadly nightshade, henbane, and datura *(D. stramonium* or *D. metel);* alternatively, it is reported that the recipe was made with datura, henbane, and mandrake. He smeared his forehead and armpits and in a brief time fell deeply asleep, waking after about twenty-four hours. In his report of the experience, he described visions of terrifying faces appearing before his eyes, wild dreams with the sensation of flying for miles through the air, periodically falling down at high speed and going up again, of landing on top of mountains, participation in dances, orgiastic feasts with sexual excesses, and participation in rituals with diabolical creatures. The active ingredients are deadly nightshade, henbane, thornapple, and mandrake.

Various Magical Oneirogenic Plants

The following list is of the most popular plants with alleged oneirogenic properties employed in modern-day magic:

Achillea millefolium

Yarrow. Opens intuitive realms by enhancing dreams. It contains cineol, bornil acetate, and acetic acid esters.

Allium cepa

Onion. Ingested onions can promote prophetic dreams. They contain tryptophan, thiamine, choline, melatonin, and kaempferol.

Aloysia triphylla

Lemon verbena. In a dream pillow it gives the sensation of flying in dreams. It contains limonene, geranial, and geraniol.

Artemisia dracunculoides

Russian tarragon. In a pillow it gives frightening dreams. The phytochemical data haven't been found, but it could contain the compounds present in *Artemisia dracunculus,* in particular thujone, elemicin, eugenol and derivatives, and linalool.

Artemesia vulgaris

Mugwort. In a pillow it helps in the remembering of dreams. In one report the participant pressed the leaves to his face and had a night filled with obscure and unclear dreams. It contains thujone, cineol, pinene, and amyrine.

Calendula officinalis

Marigold. Induces prophetic dreams. It contains caryophyllene, kaempferol, narcissin, calendine, calendol, calendrin, and calenduladiol.

Cinnamomum camphora

Camphor. Encourages daydreaming and probably also night dreaming. It contains camphor, safrole, eugenol, kaempferol, *bis*-abolol, camphene, carvacrol, α-pinene, and limonene.

Cinnamomum zeylanicum

Cinnamon. In a pillow it is proven to bring on erotic dreams. It contains caryophyllene, phellandrene, pinene, cineol, and eugenol.

Cymbopogon citratus

Lemongrass. In a pillow it soothes and creates an exotic feeling in dreams. It contains cineol, pinene, caryophyllene, citral, citronellal, citronellol, geraniol, linalool, and limonene.

Jasminum officinale

Jasmine. In a pillow it induces exotic and romantic dreams. It contains eugenol.

Laurus nobilis

Laurel. It is believed that the leaves intensify dreams. It contains eugenol, linalool, cineol, pinene, phellandrene, and geraniol.

Mentha spp.

Mint. In a pillow it adds clarity, color, and vivid images to dreams. When combined with chamomile in a tea, it is helpful in remembering dreams. It contains limonene, menthol, and menthone.

Mentha piperita

Peppermint. Burned before bed for prophetic dreams, it stimulates daydreaming and probably also night dreaming. It contains d-menthol, menthone, menthenone, menthene, piperitone, and cineol.

Nepeta cataria

Catnip. In infusion, it induces dreams. It contains nepetalactone, dihydronepetalactone, isodihydronepetalactone, and actinidine.

Pimpinella anisum

Anise. Burned on charcoal before bed it will promote prophetic dreams. It contains anethole and methylcavicol.

Pinguicula vulgaris

Common butterwort. In Norway people believed that girls would dream of their future husbands if the plant was put under their pillows. Psychoactive components aren't known for this plant.

Plantago lanceolata

Ribwort plantain. A tea in the evening may induce vivid dreams. Its composition could be similar to that of *P. major.*

Plantago major

Greater plantain. A tea in the evening may induce vivid dreams. It contains aucubin, choline, and thiamine.

Rosa spp.

Rose. In a pillow it gives peaceful dreams. It contains an essential oil, but the phytochemical data haven't been found.

Salvia officinalis

Common sage. In a pillow it creates a lost feeling or sense of imprisonment in dreams. It contains thujone.

Salvia sclarea

Clary sage. The effects of this plant include vivid dreams, dream recollection and enhancement of the dream state. It contains thujone.

Tanacetum vulgare

Tansy. In a pillow it gives violent and terrifying dreams. It contains thujone, tanacetine, tanacetone, camphor, and borneol.

Thymus spp.

Thyme. In a pillow it encourages dreams of creativity and flight, and combined with rosemary it is said to induce lucid dreams. It contains thymol, borneol, linalool, cymol, cineol, carvacrol, pinene, and menthene.

Dream Blends

Some of the magical oneirogenic plants are used in preparations known as "dream blends." Following are some reported recipes.

Peppermint, mugwort, damiana *(Turnera aphrodisiaca)*, chamomile *(Matricaria chamomilla)*, gotu kola *(Centella asiatica)*, rosemary *(Rosmarinus officinalis)*, and rose petals. Prepare a water infusion. This formula is based on an ancient formula said to evoke powerful and colorful dreams.

Sandalwood *(Santalum album)*, bergamot *(Citrus bergamia)*, ylang ylang *(Cananga odorata)*, juniper *(Juniperus osteosperma* and *Juniperus scopulorum)*, blue tansy *(Tanacetum annuum)*, tangerine *(Citrus nobilis)*, black pepper *(Piper nigrum)*, and anise. Diffuse or apply on forehead, ears, throat, eyebrows, and base of neck.

½ cup chamomile, ½ cup mint, ½ cup rose petals; add a few drops of chamomile essential oil or clary sage. To experience exotic dreams, add cinnamon or cloves *(Syzygium aromaticum)*. Prepare a pillow for soothing dreams when you want to just get away from the world at hand and create worlds of your own.

4 whole cloves, 1 tablespoon mint, 1 cinnamon stick, ½ cup rosemary, ½ cup lavender *(Lavandula officinalis)*, ½ cup rose petals. Add a few drops of jasmine essential oil to experience romantic dreams. Insert mixture into a pillow.

½ cup lemon verbena, ½ cup rosemary, ½ cup clary sage, ½ cup hops *(Humulus lupulus)*. Add a few drops of frankincense *(Boswellia sacra)* essential oil in order to enjoy creative dreams. Insert mixture into a pillow.

The compounds contained in the above-cited species are the following:

- *Boswellia sacra:* borneol, camphene, cymene, cadinene, pinene, phellandrene, limonene, verbenon, verbenol, dipentene, and olibanol
- *Cananga odorata:* safrole and eugenol
- *Centella asiatica:* humulene, pinene, bisabolene, caryophyllene, camphor, cineol, geraniol, kaempferol, limonene, linalool, myrcene, phellandrene, and thiamine
- *Citrus bergamia* and *Citrus nobilis:* the phytochemical data aren't known, but it could contain compounds present in other *Citrus* species, such as limonene, citral, citronellal, and linalool
- *Humulus lupulus:* myrcene, caryophyllene, and humulene
- *Juniperus osteosperma* and *J. scopulorum:* camphene, cadinene, juniperol, juniperine, junene, sabinene, and α-pinene
- *Lavandula officinalis:* cineol, pinene, limonene, geraniol, borneol, and linalool
- *Matricaria chamomilla:* α-bisabolol, α-bisabolol oxides A and B, and matricin
- *Piper nigrum:* cineol, limonene, pinene, caryophyllene, phellandrene, biasabolene, bisabolol, camphor, kaempferol, linalool, eugeol, safrole, myristicin, choline, acetylcholine, and thiamine
- *Rosmarinus officinalis:* camphor, camphene, borneol, thymol, linalool, cineol, and pinene
- *Santalum album:* santene, santalene, santenone, santenal, and santalon
- *Syzygium aromaticum:* eugenol, acetyleugenol, kaempferol, caryophyllene, and humulene
- *Tanacetum annuum:* the phytochemical data aren't known, but it could contain the compounds present in *Tanacetum vulgare*
- *Turnera aphrodisiaca:* cineol, α- and β-pinene, p-cymene, and caffeine.

The numerous plants used in the practice of magical beliefs are widespread throughout the world. They are generally psychoactive species and have various effects, above all hallucinogenic, but also oneirogenic properties have been attributed to some species. The use of oneirogenic species in magical practices seems likely, mostly in the context of ancient European witchcraft, based on the composition of potions and ointments and the descriptions of the effects reported in the literature of that period.

Most of the ingredients of witches' brews or magical potions attributed with oneirogenic properties in historical texts have definite psychoactive properties, such as the *Solanaceous* plants including belladona, henbane, and mandrake. The dream-inducing or dream-enhancing activity of herbs used in dream blends in herbal medicine may have psychoactive properties characterized as oneirogenic activity, but the pharmacology of the chemical constitutents of most of these plants remains to be verified in future psychopharmacological bioassays (autoexperiments).

6

Myco-Oneirogenica
Mushrooms

More than one hundred fifty psychoactive species of mushrooms are known. These species are found all over the world. They belong to different genera and are classified in three distinct biochemical classes, according to the identity of the active compounds produced. They are the Isoxazolic class, the Psilocybian class, and mushrooms characterized by the presence of lysergic acid derivatives.

The Isoxazolic class produces ibotenic acid and muscimol and is represented by species of the genus *Amanita* (above all *Amanita muscaria* and *A. pantherina*).

The Psilocybian class is more widespread, both in number of species and geographical distribution. It comprises mushrooms that synthesize the indole compounds psilocybin, psilocin, and baeocystin. Such species belong principally to the genera *Psilocybe*. (*Psilocybe [Stropharia] cubensis, P. cyanescens,* and *P. semilanceata* are among the most important.) Other species in the genera *Psilocybe* are *Panaeolus (Panaeolus subbalteatus, P. cyanescens), Inocybe (Inocybe aeruginascens), Gymnopilus (Gymnopilus spectabilis),* and *Pluteus (Pluteus salicinus).*

The last class of psychoactive mushrooms includes species that synthesize indole compounds derived from lysergic acid. They include the genera *Claviceps, Aspergillus,* and *Penicillium.* They are parasitic mushrooms that infest the gramineous plants. One of the most widely known and studied species is *Claviceps purpurea.* Its sclerotium (ergot) is parasitic on rye, wheat, barley, and other cultivated grains. It also infests wild grasses. In Europe during the Middle Ages it caused serious collective intoxications know as "St. Anthony's Fire," or ergotism.

Amanita muscaria

Experience with *A. muscaria* can be divided into three phases. In the first, nausea and possible vomiting are predominant. In the second phase, the narcotic effect prevails. The third phase is characterized by visionary content. The narcotic effect can manifest itself at different intensity levels. During sleep there can be lucid dreams and dreams with brilliant colors. The psychoactive effect of smoking *A. muscaria* is also perceptible during sleep, influencing dreams. The red dried pellicle is smoked in North America.

The active principles of *A. muscaria* are the isoxazolic alkaloids, ibotenic acid, and muscimol. Muscimol is considered five to ten times more potent than the isoxazolic alkaloids and results from a decarboxylation process of ibotenic acid during the drying process. The concentration of these compounds is greater in specimens collected in summer than those collected in autumn, and greater in young specimens rather than adult ones. The concentration is also higher in the flesh layer of the cap just under the cuticle. It seems likely that other compounds contribute to the effect of this mushroom.

Besides the subspecies, varieties, and forms of *A. muscaria,* other species of *Amanita* contain the isoxazolic alkaloids: *A. pantherina* (more potent but also more toxic than *A. muscaria*), *A. regalis, A. strobiliformis,* and probably *A. gemmata.* For this latter species the analytical results are contradictory, perhaps due to experimentation with different varieties and forms.

In every case *A. gemmata* must be considered as a suspect species; fatalities have occurred after its ingestion.

Psilocybian Mushrooms

It has been reported that psilocybian mushrooms can induce significant dreams,[1] and one species, *P. semilanceata*, is even called the "mushroom of dream." Such oneirogenic effects could be caused by methylated tryptamines.

Lycoperdon spp.

In 1961 the researches of Wasson and Heim on hallucinogenic mushrooms in the Mixtec area of Oaxaca, Mexico, led to the identification of *Lycoperdon mixtecorum* and *L. marginatum* as "narcotic" and dream-inducing species, according to the statements of the informant Agapito. The two species are known as *gi' i wa* ("first-class mushroom") and *gi' i sawa* ("second-class mushroom"), respectively, the first being more potent than the second. According to the informant, half an hour after the ingestion of a pair of specimens he could hear voices and echoes in a semi-somnolent state. It was as if the mushroom spoke to him, answering questions, predicting a disease and its outcome.

During field investigations between 1974 and 1975, Agapito identified not fewer than eleven species of narcotic dream-inducing mushrooms; among them were *Agrocybe semiorbicularis, Astraeus hygrometricus, L. marginatum, L. mixtecorum, L. oblongiosporum, Rhizopogon* sp., *Scleroderma verrucosum, Vascellum curtisii, V. intermedium,* and *V. pratense.* In particular, *A. semiorbicularis* is morphologically very similar to *Psilocybe mexicana,* a psychoactive species ritually used by Mixtecs. Agapito probably misidentified it. (The active principle psilocybin was isolated in a species of the same genus, *Agrocybe farinacea* from Japan.) Ott autoexperimented with the species at the doses prescribed by the informant, but there wasn't any psychoactive effect, only nausea and gastrointestinal problems.

Samples of all the species indicated by Agapito (with the exception of *A. semiorbicularis* and *Rhizopogon* sp.) were analyzed by means of chromatography. A search was made for psilocybin, ibotenic acid, and also *bis*-noryangonin (then considered to be the active principle of the mushroom *Gymnopilus spectabilis*), but with negative results. It was then hypothesized that the presence of not well-identified indole compounds might be found in some species of *Lycoperdon*.

The conclusion was that such mushrooms were inactive at the doses prescribed. However some activity could be possible at greater dosages, such as that reported from the United States in 1869 regarding "narcotic influence" after an abundant meal of *Lycoperdon* mushrooms. Moreover, it is possible to find reports about the presumed oneirogenic activity of other *Lycoperdon* species; this is the case with *L. pyriforme*.[2]

L. pyriforme can induce a short, and in some cases, potent narcosis. Basque witches possibly used it. One evening an experimenter ate twenty to thirty small young specimens fried in oil. The subject felt an unnatural sense of satiety followed by problems of indigestion, belches, aerophagia, and a pronounced mental stimulation. During the night oneiric stimulation was of a different quality in respect to that obtained with *C. zacatechichi* or *L. virosa*. Dreams were animated, intense, and complex, with highly varied content and lasting throughout the night. The person awoke at regular intervals, always feeling instantaneously and perfectly awake. Hearing was intensified, though sounds were neither high nor troublesome and there was not any perception of voices or echoes. With eyes closed, the subject noticed geometrical models. In the morning a sense of reinvigoration and vitality followed. The perception of more intense colors and complex geometrical models and an intensified sense of hearing persisted. This condition continued after the person fell asleep again and awoke repeatedly. The subject was left feeling weak for several days.

L. perlatum is considered edible when young, but it has a narcotic effect when old. The soporific effect is exploited by the Flathead Indians of Montana who put the spores of the *Lycoperdon* on their children's faces to make them sleep.

Boletus manicus

B. manicus is found in the Wahgi Valley in the Western Highlands of Papua New Guinea and is known among the Kuma people as *nonda gegwants nyimbil* ("left-handed penis"). The use of nonda mushrooms was first reported from the Mount Hagen area of the Western Highlands; they were considered a quasi-narcotic or stimulant, making the user temporarily insane and agitated. The mushroom is used before going out to kill another native, or in times of great excitement, anger, or sorrow. Among the Kuma people, this condition is known as *komugl taï* ("shivering madness") and for the women *ndaadl* ("mushroom delirium").

B. manicus has been reported to contain indole substances. Hofmann detected trace amounts of three indole substances, and Roger Heim has suggested that these indoles could be psychotropic. As a result, Heim conducted three bioassays with weak doses (less than 60 mg) and suggested that the amounts were insufficient to make any definite deductions. However, in a second trial ingestion was followed by the appearance of several luminous, fleeting visions during a dream. But the presence, identity, and concentration of such indoles, or other compounds, have not been proven.

Indole A, indole B, and indole C are the proposed names for the three indole chemical compounds identified by Hofmann in *B. manicus* samples. These compounds are collectively known as "manicines." The etymology of this chemical name is derived from a conflation of the Greek *manikós* ("insane") and the French noun suffix *–ine* for chemical terms, especially in basic substances.

Evidence for the presence of indoles in *B. manicus* can be found in the auditory and visual effects of nonda mushrooms. After ingesting a species of nonda, most likely *B. manicus,* Kuma men experienced Lilliputian hallucinations of bush-demons flying about their heads. One Kuma man who had eaten nonda reported that these demons also made a strange and terrible noise inside his ears. Psilocybin and other tryptamines often produce a similar buzzing noise. The Kuma regarded bush-demons as tiny, two-dimensional, and often transparent creatures.

They always identified cartoon figures readily and positively as representations of bush-demons. Kuma bush-demons were seen, heard, or felt to be any size up to the length of a person's forearm and could be either fat or thin. However, during komugl taï, bush-demons were supposed to be about the same size and proportions as wild bees. Ethnopsychiatrist Sir B. G. Burton-Bradley has claimed that the Kuma's nonda-induced hallucinations of bush-demons are more bizarre than any other description of bush-demons elsewhere in Papua New Guinea. Lilliputian hallucinations have also been experienced with the ludible use of some tryptamines.

Parasitic Mushrooms

In his previously cited work Piobb reports the preparation of a lotion to obtain prophetic dreams. It is composed of ergot (the principal ingredient), turpentine, wild duck yolk, diascordium (?), red roses, milk of she-goat or mare, ivy *(H. helix),* alchimilla (*Alchemilla* spp.?), vervain (*Verbena* sp.?), scraping of deer-horns, aconite (*Aconitum* spp.), and fat of whale. The ingredients are cooked in alcohol with camphor *(C. camphora),* coral syrup, "black root," balsam, and ammoniac and dissolved in malmsey. The lotion is smeared on hands, feet, head, and stomach before going to bed.

The psychoactive effect of the preparation is mainly due to the presence of ergot, but plants such as ivy could also add to the effect (via saponins, for example, α-hederine), as could vervain and aconite (aconitine). Some ingredients probably modulate the principal psychoactive effect, while others have no pharmacological purpose but serve secondary functions as thickening agents, to increase the absorption of active principles, or as fillers and excipients. It is also possible that some of the ingredients were included only for "magical purposes" to induce suggestion and sensationalism.

The beginning of the interest in the biochemistry of psychoactive mushrooms can be traced back to the discovery of the ritual use of mushrooms in Mexico by Wasson and the investigations carried out by

Hofmann, resulting in the identification of the active principles psilo-cybin and psilocin. Although the chemo-taxonomical research in this field is in constant and rapid development, there isn't a true progress in the study of mushroom chemistry and in the identification of new active principles. Undoubtedly, this research is not finished. It is probable that in the future, by means of a specifically chemical-toxicological approach, the presence of such active principles will be displayed in various taxonomies and habitats.

7

Zoo-Oneirogenica
Animals

During the search for techniques to alter the ordinary state of consciousness, man has turned also to the animal world. In many cases, the consumption of animals with psychoactive properties is accidental, for example, the intoxications caused by the ingestion of some fish species (dream Fish) or animals fed on psychoactive plants. In other cases man can consume psychoactive animals in a conscious way. In some civilizations a particular animal was incorporated in a culture in a system of beliefs and ritual uses, such as the snails eaten by the ancient Moche of Peru and the ducks eaten by the Olmecs in Mexico. Snails and ducks eat psychoactive species, respectively the cactus *San Pedro (Trichocereus pachanoi)* and the toad *Bufo marinus.* The animal becomes sacred and a close ecological relation between man, plant, and animal is established. From the biochemical point of view, some specific active compounds have been identified; in other cases their presence is still hypothetic or speculative. In particular among the compounds produced by animals we find tryptamine derivatives such as DMT and 5-methoxy-N,N-dimethyltryptamine (5-MeO-DMT). For example, 5-MeO-DMT has been isolated from the secretions of some toads. As for the compounds assimilated by animals that render the animals themselves psychoactive, the variety could be great, according to the psychoactive plant (or animal) ingested. The reported effects are sedative, stimulating, hallucinogenic, and aphrodisiac. Among the psychoactive animals, there are also those to which oneirogenic properties are attributed.

Giraffa camelopardalis

The Humr tribe of the Baggara Arabs, living in southwest Kurdofan, Sudan, is devoted to hunting elephants and, above all, giraffes. After having killed a giraffe, they prepare a visionary beverage known as *umm nyolokh,* employing both the liver and the bone marrow of the animal. It seems that the aim of their hunting is precisely the preparation of this beverage and not to procure food.

Drinking the beverage is supposed to cause a true obsession with giraffes. Its effects are characterized by drunkenness and the induction of dreams in which giraffes explain where more real giraffes might be found and hunted for a new preparation of the same beverage, in order to give more hallucinations with the same content. Thus those who drink umm nyolokh just once spend the rest of their lives hunting giraffes.

It is important to note that the Humr, being Mahdists, are abstemious and never get drunk with alcoholic beverages, but in the particular case of the umm nyolokh the term used is *sakran,* that is to say "drunk." According to some anthropologists, this drink is not a genuine hallucinogen and the effect is not produced by any active principle. Instead the action is induced by the unconscious, or through social conventions. In other words tribal rules of social life dictate the expectation of visionary states after the ingestion of the beverage. According to another hypothesis, the psychoactive effect is attributed to the presence of endogenous tryptamines in the bone marrow of the animal.

Dream Fish

Also known as *nightmare fish,* the *dream fish* corresponds to several fish species widespread from Hawaii to South Africa. In the Pacific Ocean, near Norfolk Island in Melanesia, one such fish is known as *Kyphosus fuscus* (silver drummer-fish) or *Kyphosus vaigiensis* (brass bream), whose ingestion causes terrifying nightmares.

In 1960 its properties were discussed in an issue of *National Geographic* magazine. Photographer Joe Roberts ate a portion of the grilled fish. The next morning he told of dreams that were pure science fiction. He dreamed of a new type of car and saw images of monuments testifying to the first travel of man into space.[1] The author of the article tried the fish and also had bizarre dreams. He ordered himself not to dream but didn't succeed. He dreamed of being at a party where everyone was naked and the orchestra played a song entitled "Yes, We Don't Have Pajamas."[2]

The active compound or compounds have not yet been identified, but the presence of tryptamine derivatives is presumed. These might include DMT, 5-MeO-DMT or 5-hydroxy-N,N-dimethyltryptamine (5-OH-DMT, bufotenine) (5). DMT and 5-MeO-DMT are not orally active, except in combination with MAOI compounds. A toxin known as ichthyoallyeinotoxin has been identified in species of *Kyphosus*; this toxin is a thermostable compound, principally localized in the head (particularly in the brain) and in the bone marrow of the animal. In Japan such fish are considered to be a culinary delicacy; no deadly intoxication has ever been documented.

In Hawaii, *Kyphosus cinerascens* (pilot fish) and *Acanthurus sandvicensis* (surgeon fish) also seem to have oneirogenic effects when ingested. The presence of ichthyoallyeinotoxin was also reported in these species.

Mullets

An oneirogenic effect has been reported from some species of mullets such as *Mugil cephalus* (flathead mullet, Tropics), *Mulloidichthys samoensis* (golden goat-fish, Indonesia), *Neomyxus chaptalli* (*uoua* mullet, Indonesia), and *Upeneus arge* (goat fish, Indonesia). This dream-inducing effect is so clearly reported that some researchers at the University of Hawaii have proposed the specific expression "ichthyosarcephialtilepsis" or more simply "hallucinatory mullet intoxication."

In particular *U. arge* of Hawaii (popularly known as *weke pahala* or *nightmare-weke*), in 1927, caused delirium and mental paralysis to some unwitting Japanese workers who ate the fish. Hallucinations attributed to *U. arge* have also been reported on Kauai and Molokai in the Hawaiian Islands, where it seems that the active compound found in the fish occurs only in the period from June to August. The effect seems to be rather variable from one person to another. Some aren't affected; others are intoxicated and have nightmares; while still others experience pleasant hallucinations. There are varying beliefs about what part of the fish causes intoxication, ranging from the entire fish, to the head, brain, or tail. To confuse matters, there is a nontoxic variety of this species, difficult to distinguish from the toxic one and ingested without any effect.

It had been hypothesized that the effect was caused by a psychosomatic phenomenon, an allergic reaction, a bacterial contamination, or also (according to some fishermen) due to the fact that *U. arge* eats a particular species of alga.

Marcus Berger has reported that ichthyoallyeinotoxin would have been identified in *U. arge* and in the other above-cited species.

Bamboo Worm

The use of this larval insect to induce ecstatic sleep is cited by a nineteenth-century French explorer, Augustin de Saint-Hilaire, in a passage contained in reports written about his travels to South America. After his return to France from a trip to Brazil between 1816 and 1823, the author published geographical, ethnological, and naturalistic data describing the customs of the native Malalis of eastern Brazil in the Minas Gerais Province.

He reports that the insect lives in the bamboo trunk (but only when the plant is flowering) and that it is locally known as *bicho da tacuara* ("bamboo worm"). Following the opinion of an entomologist of that period, the author assigned the bamboo worm to the genus *Cossus* or *Hepiale*. Today the bicho da tacuara corresponds to the larva of the moth *Myelobia smerintha*. The larva lives on such bamboos as *Guadua* sp.

(taquarassu), Merostachys neesii (taquara poca), M. rideliana (taquara lixa), and *Nastes barbatus* and feeds in the internodes of the plant.

According to the French explorer, such insects are considered an excellent food and some Portuguese, living among the natives, cooked them on the fire until an oily mass suitable for preservation was formed. The Malalis consider the head of the insect poisonous, and the author reports having seen the locals in possession of only dried insects without the heads. The same explorer, following the instructions of a local guide, ate the insect after having separated the head and the intestinal tube, appreciating the very pleasant and creamy taste. The bicho da tacuara was said to have a medicinal use, as vulnerary in the form of dried and ground specimens, as well as a psychotropic use.

In this latter case, the insect is dried and consumed minus the head, but without discarding the intestinal tube; in fact, according to the Malalis, the intestinal tube is the only portion capable of producing a narcotic effect. The author describes this particular use by the natives and the Portuguese residing in the area. When strong emotion makes them sleepless, they swallow the dried worms without the head but with the intestinal tube. They fall into an ecstatic sleep that often lasts for more than a day. This experience is similar to taking an excessive amount of opium. On awakening, subjects related marvelous dreams; they saw splendid forests, ate delicious fruits, and killed the choicest game without difficulty. The Malalis added that they rarely indulged in this debilitating pleasure.[3]

Even though the name *bicho da tacuara* is still used today, it seems that the intoxicant effect has been forgotten. There aren't any chemical-pharmacological data concerning the bamboo worm. According to some researchers (and the report of De Saint-Hilaire), it would seem that the active substance isn't destroyed during the drying process and is contained in the salivary glands or intestinal tube. Another possibility is that the active compound is found in the bamboo, and the insect merely assimilates that compound from the plant, concentrating it in its tissues.

The research on the human use of psychoactive animals is not well developed and is characterized by nonsystematic and isolated studies.

The available data are essentially represented by modern ethnographic field researches, travel reports of past explorers, texts of ancient literatures, and archaeological and iconographic evidences. There are also neither verified nor verifiable evidences of autoexperimentations, in some cases almost anecdotal. The interdisciplinary research on psychoactive animals could represent one of the most promising fields of investigation in relation to the origin and distribution of psychoactive substances in nature.

8

Bromato-Oneirogenica

Foods

The idea of dream as a "deceit" derived from a bad physiological state is reported by Aristotle in *De insomnis,* where the oneiric production is linked to old age and to the ingestion of certain foods. This belief in the physiological and gastronomic origin of dream is above all typical of Greek medicine as expressed in the *Corpus Hippocraticum,* and it was followed up in the Renaissance under the influence of the writings of Galen.

In the thirteenth century many authors thought that dreams originated from an organic lack of balance due to internal or external causes. It was believed that indigestible foods or fever could induce demonic visions. However, with a favorable mood or agreeable foods, it was possible to see angels and saints. In the 1500s, according to Cardano in *De subtilitate rerum,* eating cabbages, beans, garlic, or onions render the dreams gloomy, agitated, or dreadful. Della Porta in *Magia naturalis* reports that witches abuse certain natural substances whose action would be helped by eating chestnuts, beans, legumes, and roots.

In more recent times eating indigestible foods before going to sleep was also thought to favor oneiric activity. Generally such phenomenon was considered accidental, but various artists and writers voluntarily employed this technique for creative research, a practice common during the Romantic era.

Around the beginning of the 1800s, evening meetings were fashionable where participants ate great quantities of food in order to induce nocturnal nightmares, which they then described to each other. This fashion found its expression in the European visionary arts between the end of the eighteenth and the beginning of the nineteenth century. Among its representatives was the Swiss artist Johann Füssli (1741–1825), one of the most important inspirations of Romanticism. Before going to sleep, Füssli would eat great quantities of raw meat, and according to some scholars, the fantastic subjects of his paintings were inspired by this dream-inducing practice.

Ann Radcliffe (1764–1823), author of gothic novels, ate raw carrots before going to sleep, while other writers of the same literary genre ate rotten meat with the aim of evoking terrifying images. Other literary works supposedly created after nocturnal alimentary indigestion are *Frankenstein* by Mary Shelley (1798–1851), *The Strange Case of Doctor Jekyll and Mister Hyde* by Robert Louis Stevenson (1850–1894), and *Dracula* by Bram Stoker (1847–1912). It seems that *Dracula* was inspired by an ingestion of crawfish. In an interview in 1970, the author Anaïs Nin stated that when she was in Paris she and her friends ate cheese before going to sleep in order to induce dreams. According to some popular beliefs, seasoned cheese and watercress are the proper foods to be eaten late in the evening in order to experience lively and lucid dreams. This supposed dream-inducing property of cheese is worth considering.

A study carried out by the British Cheese Board, "Cheese & Dreams Study," reveals that eating cheese before bed will not only aid a good night's sleep but also different cheeses will, in fact, cause various types of dreams.[1] Six different types of British cheese were given to an equal number of participants: Stilton, Cheddar, Red Leicester, British Brie, Lancashire, and Cheshire. During one week, each participant ate a 20-gram piece of cheese thirty minutes before going to sleep and recorded the type of sleep and dreams that they experienced. Stilton produced vivid, bizarre dreams, although none were described as bad experiences; highlights included talking soft toys, elevators that moved sideways, a vegetarian crocodile upset because it could not eat children, dinner party guests being traded for camels, soldiers fighting with each other using kittens instead of guns, and a party in a psychiatric hospital. Those eating British Brie had very nice dreams but also rather odd, obscure ones, such as driving against a battleship or having a drunken conversation with a dog. Cheshire cheese did not produce many dreams.

In a bioassay Gianluca Toro ingested a good portion of cheese before going to bed. During the night there was continuous and complex oneiric activity with colored images.

According to anecdotal reports, other foods that supposedly affect dreaming after ingestion (probably in great quantity) are bananas, cereals, and milk. Foods that increase the chances of having more vivid or also lucid dreams include mustard and ice cream (reported as affecting the frequency of lucid dreaming), yogurt, chocolate, sardines, anchovies (containing deanol, a substance promoting lucid dreams), and pickled onions.[2]

There is also a mysterious hypothetical illness in the Philippines known as "sudden unexplained nocturnal death syndrome," or locally as *bangugot*. This syndrome is supposedly induced by immoderately eating contaminated food before sleeping, with terrifying nightmares and cardiac collapse due to fright, accompanied by the distorted twisting of facial features.

As to a possible explanation for the dream-inducing data found in this chapter, one must realize that most of the evidence comes from anecdotal reports, in many cases poorly referenced. Romantic period physicians and nineteenth-century scientists generally interpreted nightmares as a consequence of natural troubles caused by undigested humors present in the stomach that evaporated to the brain. Indigestion might lead to waking and this could be associated with better dream recall, which could be interpreted as linked to the ingestion of food.

Another explanation is that food-induced dreams are the result of a placebo effect, a sort of self-fulfilling prophecy. It has been proposed that eating abundantly before falling asleep compels the digestive system to intense activity with probable oneiric repercussions. From a biochemical point of view, some foods could contain compounds (amino acids and vitamins) that influence the dream process if taken before bedtime.

Generally, the accidental manifestation of perceptive troubles as a consequence of the ingestion of certain foods before bed is quite common, both in everyday life and in medical literature. The knowledge of the influence of food on dream production is widespread but is often disregarded. Bromato-oneiorgenica could be worth considering in order to gain a better understanding of the role of external factors on dream production.

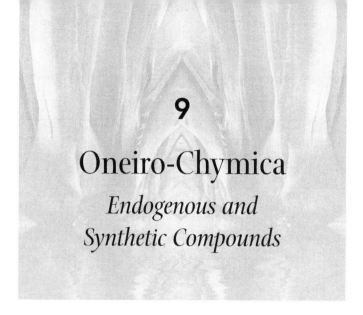

9

Oneiro-Chymica

Endogenous and
Synthetic Compounds

Compounds with possible oneirogenic properties can be found naturally in the human body. They could be our physiological oneirogens, and some of them (the methylated tryptamines) have a counterpart in plants, mushrooms, and animals. On the other hand, there are synthetic compounds with an oneirogenic effect that generally manifests itself as a side effect. Synthetic compounds can be designed in a laboratory in order to produce a certain pharmacological response.

Oneirogens Produced within the Body

The endogenous presence of psychoactive substances such as DMT, 5-MeO-DMT, and bufotenine in human beings isn't definitively demonstrated. From the chemical-analytical point of view, many factors can influence their detection in the human body; their presence has been repeatedly confirmed and denied.

One of the first studies on the biosynthesis of these tryptamines dates back to the mid-1950s, when it was proposed that bufotenine and its monomethyl derivative were formed from the neurotransmitter serotonin. On the basis of available data, the biosynthetic pathways proposed for DMT, 5-MeO-DMT, and bufotenine involve tryptophan from the diet and a series of enzymic reactions:

tryptophan → decarboxylation → tryptamine → methylation →
DMT

tryptophan → hydroxylation → 5-hydroxytryptophan (5-HTP) →
decarboxylation → 5-hydroxytryptamine (5-HT, serotonin)→
N-methylation → 5-OH-DMT (bufotenine)

5-OH-DMT→ N-methylation → 5-MeO-DMT

Alternatively:

DMT → hydroxylation → 5-MeO-DMT

At the beginning of the 1950s the presence of such methylated tryptamines in the body was proposed as a cause for mental illnesses (schizophrenia, for example). Such compounds were found not only in psychotic patients but also in persons not affected by mental illness. It was hypothesized that these compounds might have another unknown role in the brain.

β-carbolines can be biosynthesized by the body starting from primary tryptamines, such as tryptamine, serotonin, and 5-methoxytryptamine. At the beginning of the 1980s, 6-methoxytetrahydro-β-carboline (6-MeO-THβC, pinoline) was identified in the pineal gland in concentration similar to that of melatonin. The proposed reactions for its biosynthesis are the following:

5-HT → cyclization → 6-hydroxytetrahydroβ-carboline
(6-OH-THβC) → Pinoline

5-HT → 5-MeO-tryptamine → cyclization → pinoline

Other important endogenous β-carbolines are 1-methyl-β-carboline (1-Me-βC), 2-methyl-β-carboline (2-Me-βC), and 1-methyltetrahydroβ-carboline (1-Me-THβC).

DMT and 5-MeO-DMT are not orally active except in the presence of MAOI compounds. Until recent times the psychoactivity of bufotenine was not well defined. Taken orally it didn't produce any psychoactive effect. Even snuffed as a pure compound it showed no determined activity (only fever, flushing, lachrymation, tachycardia, and tachypnea). When bufotenine was taken intravenously it had high toxicity characterized by cardiopulmonary problems. It also produced psychoactive activity comparable to that of DMT and 5-MeO-DMT. When taken intermuscularly bufotenine produced unconfirmed visionary effects with perception of color plays, lights, and geometrical forms. Other reports of visionary experiences concern experiments with snuffing powders based on *Anadenanthera* spp., in particular *A. colubrina* var. *cebil* and *A. peregrina* var. *peregrina*. Bufotenine would be the only relevant alkaloid present in the ripe seeds of the two above-cited species of *Anadenanthera*. It has been reported that these seeds induce a sense of depersonalization, mystery and numinous consciousness, a sensation of having a "sixth sense," and visions of sinuous multicolored doodled patterns, first with closed eyes, then on surfaces. Recently Ott has carried out a series of personal psychonautic assays with bufotenine, reproducing the use of snuffing psychoactive powders in shamanic contexts. Ott also consumed bufotenine by intranasal, sublingual, oral, intrarectal, and pulmonary administration. He found the compound to be psychoactive for all of these experimented approaches, depending on dose. In particular, the intrarectal activity was verified in combination with an MAOI compound.

Dr. J. C. Callaway has proposed that the visual and emotional phenomena of dreams could be produced by the joint action of β-carbolines and methylated tryptamines. During a dream the concentration of β-carbolines would increase, inhibiting the MAO enzymes and favoring the action of methylated tryptamines. On the other hand, the receptors of a cerebral area concerned in REM phases of sleep have shown a high affinity for pinoline. According to Rifat, the serotonergic 5-HT_{2A} receptors seem to be involved in the initiation and termination of dreams, with the action of DMT and related compounds acting as endogenous 5-HT_{2A} agonists. Such compounds could be involved in other processes meant to sustain the high metabolic activity found in oneiric phenomena, and DMT in particular would be cyclically produced or used during REM phases.[1]

Other compounds possibly related to the process of dream production are N-acetyl-5-methoxytryptamine (melatonin), endopsychosin (angeldustin) and 2,2-dimethylaminoethanol (DMAE, deanol).

Melatonin is a hormone produced by the pineal gland. Light induces melatonin production, while darkness inhibits it. Melatonin principally regulates the cycle of dream and waking, the behavioral equilibrium, and some mental functions. Melatonin could reduce the latency period of REM sleep and increase its quantity and duration. It seems that high doses administered before bedtime induce vivid dreams.[2]

Endopsychosin is a term indicating a not yet identified neurotransmitter. Endopsychosin would simulate the psychoactive effects of phencyclidine (PCP, angeldustin), a dissociative anaesthetic, and would be produced during stress periods, leading to an oneiric and detached condition. It could be a substance that simulates a fever state (hallucinations, in particular), above all characterized by dysphoria, perception of Lilliputians, and geometrical and linear forms and could be involved in dream production in general.

Deanol is present in human brains in low concentration. It is a precursor of acetylcholine. This compound could increase the frequency of lucid dreams and could be hypothetically involved in their induction.[3]

Adrenochrome is a derivative of adrenaline. Adrenochrome is formed by enzymic oxidation of adrenaline, and it is an acetylcholinesterase inhibitor. It increases the levels of acetylcholine involved in the chemistry of dreams.

Synthetic Drugs

Dissociative Anaesthetics

The dissociative anaesthetics are a class of anaesthetics that produce unresponsiveness to stimuli by dissociation of different functions of the mind. Consciousness, memory, perception, and motor activity are all dissociated from each other. The psychedelic effects of dissociative anaesthetics are nothing whatsoever like the classical hallucinogens (psilocybin, mescaline, LSD, etc.). The hallucinogens induce sensory overload, a focus on details, and an awareness of the external world, while dissociative anaesthetics induce a sensory shutdown, a focus on and awareness of the internal world. Most recreational use occurs below the anaesthetic level; among the uncommon side effects of general anaesthetics are vivid or unusual dreams, or nightmares.[4]

In the arylcyclohexylamines class, we find ketamine, phencyclidine (PCP) and analogues (PCC, PCE, PCPy, PHP, TCP), and tiletamine.[5]

Other structural classes of compounds that produce potent PCP-like effects are benz(f)isoquinolines, propanolamines (2-MDP), benzomorphans (pentazocine), dioxolanes (dexoxadrol and etoxadrol), and tricyclic compounds (MK-801 or dizocilpine). All of these compounds are known to bind at the same receptor site as PCP and share at least some of its pharmacological profile.[6]

In the group of synthetic morphine analogues we find dextromethorphan, an isomer of levorphanol (a narcotic analgesic). Although chemically related to opiates, it does not have any opiate-like effects. Its actual effects are closest to those of ketamine. It has been reported that DXM may induce lucid and very vivid dreams.[7]

Finally, we mention nitrous oxide. Its effects have been compared to those of ketamine.[8]

Other Compounds

Propofol is a potent intravenous hypnotic agent, an anaesthetic chemically unrelated to other anaesthetics. Patients who underwent total intravenous anaesthesia with propofol reported the most dreaming, as compared to patients treated with other anaesthetics.

Fenfluramine can induce a psychotomimetic state; frequent and vivid dreams were reported.[9] In a case reported by Stephen Laberge, quite large dosages of Valium (diazepam) and Panadeine Forte (a mixture of paracetamol and codeine phosphate) induced long and continuous dreams, even lucid ones.[10]

In another case, Percodan (oxycodone) induced vivid dreams. Oxycodone is a semisynthetic opium derivative, acting as a painkiller.[11]

Ether (diethyl ether) was used in the past as an anaesthetic. Often etherized patients referred to dreams during operations. Frequently those dreams pertained to early periods of their lives. Many patients dreamed that they were traveling. From a comparison of what patients express by words or gestures under the influence of ether with what they say of their dreams afterward, it appears that remembered dreams occur only when the patients are fast emerging from the second phase of anaesthesia into a state of complete consciousness.

Cholinergics, the Oneiropoietics

As we have seen, the oneiric activity in REM phases is mediated by the neurotransmitter acetylcholine. In these REM phases the excitability of acetylcholine neurons increases for the lowering of the serotonergic inhibition. The cholinergic drugs are able to increase the release of acetylcholine and theoretically could influence dream production.

The cholinergic drugs are chemical compounds that have effects similar to those of acetylcholine. In respect to the mechanism of action, they are divided into two groups. The first comprises compounds with direct action, interacting with the acetylcholine receptors by means of their structural analogy. The second group has an indirect action and are known as anticholinesterasic. They inhibit the action of cholinesterase enzymes that would otherwise metabolize acetylcholine, preventing its destruction. The inhibition could be irreversible and reversible; the difference being that the former damages the acetylcholinesterase enzyme while the latter does not. The cholinergic drugs find an important application in treating cognitive symptoms of Alzheimer's disease. The drugs commonly prescribed are donezepil, rivastigmine, and galanthamine. Tacrine is rarely prescribed today because of associated side effects.

In chemical microstimulation experiments, REM sleep was induced by means of injections of cholinergic drugs into the cerebral pontine system. Evidence showed that the structure and timing of the REM expanding effect depended on which area of the cerebral pontine system was chemically altered. REM periods were longer and more intense, with a higher number of rapid eye movements. The data on some cholinergic drugs report lucid dreams as a possible side effect. Laberge is testing minimum doses of an Alzheimer's drug on seasoned lucid dreamers and has found that nine out of ten participants had one or more lucid dreams on an active night.[12]

Cholinergic drugs and compounds include ambenonium, arecoline, bethanechol, carbachol, deanol, donezepil, echothiophate iodide, edrophonium, galanthamine, hexafluorenium bromide, huperzine A and B, isoflurophate, lobeline, metacholine, nicotine, physostigmine, pilocarpine, pyridostigmine, rivastigmine, and tacrine.[13] Some limited comments on particular compounds are worth considering.

Arecoline has been isolated from *A. catechu* (betel nut). The compound has at least a partial MAOI effect. In Africa and Polynesia betel is commonly chewed for its stimulating properties, and it forms an integral part of social life. Ground or crushed betel nuts are combined with spices and lime and then wrapped in a leaf of *Piper betle*. This use has prehistoric origins.

Lobeline has been isolated from *Lobelia* spp. *(Lobelia cardinalis, L. inflata, L. tupa)*. It has a short-term stimulating effect, but higher doses may have narcotic effects. It is said that it exerts nicotine-like activity. Among native Indians of the New World, *Lobelia* species have a medicinal, ceremonial, magical, and psychoactive use. The dried leaves are smoked alone or with tobacco. The Mapuche of Chile smoke *L. tupa* for its narcotic or inebriating effects.

Galanthamine is an alkaloid extracted from *Galanthus nivalis, G. woronowii,* and daffodil bulbs *(Narcissus pseudonarcissus)*. It is reported that daffodil bulb extract can promote lucid dreaming.[14]

Huperzine B is an experimental drug, and its effect as a dream-inducing agent has been reported in relation to *Lycopodium* spp. and to the traditional use of *L. squarrosum*.

Physostigmine is an alkaloid extracted from *Physostigma venenosum,* an extremely poisonous West African vine. The natives of Africa employ its beans (called *calabar beans* or *esere*) as an ordeal. It is given to an accused person to eat. If the person vomits within half an hour he is accounted innocent, but if he succumbs he is found guilty. Physostigmine induces REM sleep in humans and increases its frequency or duration. Results indicate that dreaming occurred during physostigmine-induced REM periods but physostigmine did not alter mentation during non-REM sleep. These dreams were similar to spontaneous REM period dreams in content, vividness, and emotionality.

Pilocarpine is extracted from *Pilocarpus pennatifolius,* a plant native to Brazil. This alkaloid mimics the action of acetylcholine. The plant, known as *jaborandi* among the Amazonian Indians, is used to induce sweating.[15]

Carbachol has the ability to induce REM sleep, while deanol increases the frequency of conscious dreams.

Other acetylcholinesterase inhibitors, which are found in experimental drugs, include the following compounds: 3-chloro-9-ethyl-6,7,8,9,10,11-hexahydro-7,11-methanocyclooocta[b]quinolin-12-amine, 3-[(1s)-1-(dimethylamino)ethyl] phenol, 1-deoxy-1-thio-heptaethylene glycol, methylphosphinic acid, methylphosphonic acid ester group, 9-N-phenyl-methylamino-tacrine, M-(N,N,N-trimethylammonio)-2,2,2-trifluoro-1,1-dihydroxyethylbenzene, and MF268 compound.[16]

Dietary Supplements: Preparing for Dreams

Some dietary supplements, taken before bedtime, can prepare the process of dream production, acting as precursors to substances involved in dream chemistry. These supplements include tryptophan, 5-HTP, amino acids such as methionine and serine, choline, and the vitamin B complex. They also help in remembering and prolonging dreams.[17]

Tryptophan and 5-HTP are part of the biosynthetic process leading to the synthesis of serotonin and methylated tryptamines, while the metabolites of serotonin are melatonin and pinoline. Methylated tryptamines, pinoline, and melatonin are compounds possibly involved in the process of dream production.

Among the amino acids, methionine and serine participate in the biosynthesis of choline. The choline is then transformed into acetylcholine, the major neurotransmitter involved in REM phases of sleep.

In the vitamin B complex, we find vitamin B_1 (thiamine), B_3 (nicotinic acid), B_5 (pantotenoic acid), B_6 (pyridoxine), B_9 (folic acid), and B_{12}

(cyanocobalamine). B_1 is involved in the biosynthesis of acetylcholine. B_3 participates in the production of serotonin, increasing the concentration of this neurotransmitter in the brain. B_5 is necessary for the synthesis of acetylcholine. B_9 and B_{12} are involved in the synthesis of the amino acid methionine. Vitamin B_6 seems to be the most effective dream inducer. It participates in the synthesis of serotonin (from tryptophan) and GABA, in the conversion of tryptophan to vitamin B_3, and in the metabolism of amino acids and biogenic amines. It is contained in potatoes, bananas, beans, nuts, red meat, yeast, eggs, carrots, peas, walnuts, spinach, rice, soybeans, lentils, avocados, turnip greens, peppers, and cauliflower. Vitamin B_6 helps with dream production and in recall, clarity, and lucidity, often in combination with melatonin or with techniques of lucid dreaming.[18]

The research on the human endogenous compounds could lead to a better understanding of the working mechanisms of our brain in general, and of those related to dreams in particular. The knowledge of our oneiric world would also benefit by specifically designed synthetic drugs as probes in psychopharmacological investigations.

Interdisciplinary Perspectives on Psychoactive Substances

Modern research in the field of psychoactive substances cannot be limited to a single science. In order to have a picture as complete as possible, it is necessary to integrate data from different disciplines of the human knowledge in an interdisciplinary approach.

This book is based on a systematic, interdisciplinary research approach to oneirogens, or dream drugs. An interdisciplinary (multidisciplinary) approach to the study of psychoactive drugs was first recommended in 1775 by August L. von Schlözer. Schlözer argued that interdisciplinary research was necessary on plant drugs and that they needed to be studied from religious, therapeutic, medicinal, sociological, economic, commercial, and financial perspectives. Later, in 1938, Dr. H. Putnam expanded an interdisciplinary approach to the study of psychoactive drugs by including the disciplines of archaeology, chemistry, theology, philology, linguistics, and ethnography.

The interdisciplinary research presented in this book draws on the disciplines of pharmacognosy, ethnopharmacology, ethnopharmacognosy, ethnobotany, ethnomycology, and entheobotany.

Pharmacognosy

Pharmacognosy is the scientific study of biologically active agents (drugs). It is the scientific discipline concerned with drugs of natural origin that affect the health of human beings or animals. Research in pharmacognosy is highly specialized, and there is a tendency to focus on sophisticated techniques of phytochemical analysis.

Ethnopharmacology

Ethnopharmacology is a nascent field of scientific inquiry based on systematic, multidisciplinary research. It is the interdisciplinary scientific exploration of biologically active agents employed or observed by human beings. The term *ethnopharmacology* was first introduced as a scientific term in 1967 at the international symposium in San Francisco, California. The "Ethnopharmacological Search for Psychoactive Drugs" symposium discussed the history, anthropology, botany, chemistry, and pharmacology of traditional psychoactive drugs. The aim of ethnopharmacology is to obtain and maintain a broad multidisciplinary perspective on the use of crude drugs and poisons in a traditional context by correlating and integrating scientific data offered by a wide variety of different disciplines, such as anthropology, archaeology, botany, chemistry, history, linguistics, medicine, pharmacology, toxicology, and zoology. Research in ethnopharmacology involves the observation, description, and experimental investigation of drugs and their biological activities.

Ethnopharmacognosy

It has been suggested that *ethnopharmacognosy* is a more appropriate term for the interdisciplinary approach of ethnopharmacology. Ethnopharmacognosy represents anthropologically informed pharmacognostic investigation combining both naturalistic field observations (participant observation) and controlled laboratory evaluation of human behavior. The aim of ethnopharmacognosy research is the analysis and explanation of traditional and contemporary drug practices based on firsthand observation and accurate description. The objectives of ethnopharmacognosy are to rescue and document an important cultural heritage before it is lost and to investigate and evaluate the drugs employed. In ethnopharmacognosy research the object of study is the directly observed behaviors of drug users and their knowledge of drugs and drug use. Drug users' behavior and knowledge is then compared with the current literature on clinical and experimental pharmacology to determine the role that chemicals play in drug users' experiences. Ethnopharmacognosy combines the ethnographic and sociological study of the subjective experience of drug users with the pharmacological approach of studying the effects of drugs.

Ethnobotany

Ethnobotany was once defined as "the study of the interrelationships between plants and humans." But the interpretation and understanding of the word *ethnobotany* has changed since it was first introduced in 1895. Ethnobotany originally referred to the distribution and dispersal of plant species and their uses by prehistoric or aboriginal populations. The present interpretation and understanding of ethnobotany is the realization of the role plants play in social organization and behavior among contemporary indigenous peoples.

Ethnobotany was defined by the late Prof. Richard E. Schultes, former director of the Botanical Museum at Harvard University, as: "The study of human evaluation and manipulation of plant materials, substances, and phenomena." Schultes asserted that ethnobotany must be highly interdisciplinary, drawing from aspects of botany, anthropology, phytochemistry, pharmacology, and other related scientific disciplines.

Ethnomycology

Ethnomycology is a nascent field of scientific inquiry described as the study of human cultural and historical interaction with fungi, especially mushrooms. It is defined as the study of the role that fungi play in past and present human cultures. Ethnomycology is a relatively new branch of ethnobotany combining the fields of anthropology (ethnography) and botany (mycology). Ethnomycological research involves the multidisciplinary scientific study of the role of fungi in human culture.

Entheobotany

Entheobotany is entheogenic ethnobotany: the science of shamanic inebriants or visionary plant drugs. *Entheogen* is a neologism that was first proposed in 1979 by Carl A. P. Ruck for states of shamanic and ecstatic possession induced by the ingestion of psychoactive drugs. Entheobotany is the multidisciplinary scientific study of the ethnopharmacognosy of entheogens.

Entheobotanical investigation comprises the following phases:

traditional ecological knowledge
ethnobotany
ethnopharmacognosy
psychonautic bioassays
phytochemistry
entheognosy

An interdisciplinary perspective is essential in order to uncover the different motivations leading traditional cultures to use a particular psychoactive substance and to understand why it is used in a certain way. The importance of phytochemical research (in constant and rapid development) in combination with psychonautic bioassays (autoexperimentations) is evident.

APPENDIX 2

Oneiropoeia
Tables

Some of the terms reported under the "Notes" column in the tables that follow refer to the type of use of the corresponding species, product, or substance. Such terms are defined as follows:

- Accidental: not voluntarily employed in order to obtain an oneirogenic effect

- Anecdotal: employment as an oneirogen based on poorly documented data

- Magical: employed as part of rituals of magic, both in ancient and modern times

- Modern: employed in modern cultures

- Possible: employment as oneirogen not completely demonstrated

- Traditional: employed by cultures that have continued their use of the substance for many years
- (--): indicates there is no common name available.

PHYTO-ONEIROGENICA: PLANTS

Name	Notes
Acacia retinoides (Swamp wattle)	Possible oneirogen
Achillea millefolium (Yarrow)	Magical
Acorus calamus (Sweet flag)	Traditional/modern, anectdotal oneirogenic activity (in combination with *V. officinalis*)
Aesculus californicus (California buckeye)	Opium substitute
Aesculus pavia (Red buckeye)	Opium substitute
Allium cepa (Onion)	Magical
Aloysia triphylla (Lemon verbena)	Magical, also in combination with other plants
Argemone mexicana (Mexican poppy)	Opium substitute
Argemone platyceras (Chicalote)	Opium substitute
Artemisia absinthium (Wormwood)	Anecdotal oneirogenic activity
Artemisia dracunculoides (Russian tarragon)	Magical
Artemisia vulgaris (Mugwort)	Magical, also in combination with other plants
Arum maculatum (Lords and Ladies)	Possible oneirogen
Asclepias syriaca (Syrian asclepias)	Possible oneirogen
Atropa belladonna (Deadly nightshade)	Traditional/magical
Ayahuasca	Traditional/modern
Bernoullia flammea (Amapola silvestre)	Opium substitute
Borago officinalis (Borage)	Anecdotal oneirogenic activity
Boswellia sacra (Frankincense)	Magical, in combination with other plants
Brugmansia spp. (Angel's trumpet)	Traditional
Calea zacatechichi (Dream herb)	Traditional/modern
Calendula officinalis (Marigold)	Magical
Cananga odorata (Ylang ylang)	Magical, in combination with other plants
Cannabis sativa (Hemp)	Traditional/modern
Casimiroa edulis (White zapote)	Traditional
Centella asiatica (Gotu kola)	Magical, in combination with other plants

PHYTO-ONEIROGENICA: PLANTS (cont'd)

Name	Notes
Cestrum spp. (Cestrum)	Possible oneirogen
Cinnamomum camphora (Camphor)	Magical
Cinnamomum zeylanicum (Cinnamon)	Magical, also in combination with other plants
Citrus bergamia (Bergamot)	Magical, in combination with other plants
Citrus nobilis (Tangerine)	Magical, in combination with other plants
Clematis virginiana (Virgin's bower)	Traditional
Curcuma longa (Curcuma)	Anecdotal oneirogenic activity
Cymbopogon citratus (Lemongrass)	Magical
Cymbopogon densiflorus (Lemongrass)	Traditional
Cyphomandra spp. (Tree tomato)	Possible oneirogen
Cypripedium calceolus (Lady's slipper)	Traditional
Datura metel (Angel's trumpet)	Traditional/magical
Datura stramonium (Thornapple)	Traditional/magical
Desfontainia spinosa (Desfontainia)	Traditional
Duboisia hopwoodii (Pituri)	Traditional, opium substitute
Duboisia myoporoides (Pituri)	Possible oneirogen
Elaeagnus sp. (Oleaster)	Traditional
Entada rheedii (African dream herb)	Traditional
Epilobium angustifolium (Rosebay)	Anecdotal oneirogenic activity
Equisetum palustre (Marsh horsetail)	Possible oneirogen
Erythrina americana (Colorines)	Traditional
Erythroxylon spp. (Coca plants)	Possible oneirogen
Eschscholzia californica (California poppy)	Opium substitute
Euphorbia spp. (Spurge)	Opium substitute
Galbulimima belgraveana (Galbulimima)	Traditional
Ginkgo biloba (Ginkgo)	Possible oneirogen
Heimia salicifolia (Sinicuiche)	Traditional/modern
Homalomena belgraveana (Ereriba)	Traditional, possible oneirogen (in combination with *G. belgraveana*)

PHYTO-ONEIROGENICA: PLANTS (cont'd)

Name	Notes
Homalomena ereriba (Ereriba)	Traditional, possible oneirogen (in combination with *G. belgraveana*)
Homalomena lauterbachii (Ereriba)	Traditional, possible oneirogen (in combination with *G. belgraveana*)
Humulus lupulus (Hop)	Magical, in combination with other plants
Hyoscyamus muticus (Egyptian henbane)	Traditional
Hyoscyamus niger (Henbane)	Traditional, magical
Ilex guayusa (Guayusa)	Traditional
Jasminum officinale (Jasmine)	Magical, also in combination with other plants
Juniperus osteosperma (Utah juniper)	Magical, in combination with other plants
Juniperus scopulorum (Mountain juniper)	Magical, in combination with other plants
Kaempferia galanga (Maraba)	Traditional
Kyphi	Magical
Lactuca quercina (Oak-leaved lettuce)	Opium substitute
Lactuca sativa (Garden lettuce)	Opium substitute
Lactuca serriola (Prickly lettuce)	Opium substitute
Lactuca virosa (Wild lettuce)	Opium substitute
Laurus nobilis (Laurel)	Magical
Lavandula officinalis (Lavender)	Magical, in combination with other plants
Litsea glutinosa (Maidalakri)	Alternative attribution for *X. spinosa*
Litsea sebifera (Maida la)	Alternative attribution for *X. spinosa*
Lycopodium cernuum (Creeping clubmoss)	Possible oneirogen
Lycopodium gnidioides (Tsilaky)	Traditional, possible oneirogen
Lycopodium selago (Fir moss)	Possible oneirogen
Lycopodium serratum (Quian ceng ta)	Possible oneirogen
Lycopodium squarrosum (Water tassel)	Traditional

PHYTO-ONEIROGENICA: PLANTS (cont'd)

Name	Notes
Mandragora autumnalis (Mandrake)	Traditional/magical
Mandragora officinarum (Mandrake)	Traditional/magical
Matricaria chamomilla (Chamomille)	Magical, in combination with other plants
Melissa officinalis (Balm)	Anecdotal oneirogenic activity
Mellitis melissophyllum (Bastard balm)	Magical, anecdotal oneirogenic activity
Mentha spp. (Mint)	Magical, also in combination with other plants
Mentha piperita (Peppermint)	Magical, also in combination with other plants
Mimosa hostilis (Jurema)	Traditional/modern
Monotropa uniflora (Indian pipe)	Opium substitute
Mucuna pruriens (Itchweed)	Possible oneirogen
Myristica fragrans (Nutmeg)	Anecdotal oneirogenic activity
Mitragynia speciosa (Kratom)	Opium substitute
Nepeta cataria (Catnip)	Traditional/magical
Nicotiana rustica (Wild tobacco)	Possible oneirogen
Nicotiana tabacum (Tobacco)	Possible oneirogen
Papaver bracteatum (Armenian poppy)	Opium substitute
Papaver rhoeas (Common poppy)	Opium substitute
Papaver somniferum (Opium poppy)	Traditional/modern
Pellaea ternifolia (Piukelawen)	Traditional, also in combination with *U. candollei*
Pimpinella anisum (Anise)	Magical, also in combination with other plants
Pinguicula vulgaris (Common butterwort)	Magical
Piper methysticum (Intoxicating pepper)	Traditional/modern, anecdotal oneirogenic activity
Piper nigrum (Black pepper)	Magical, in combination with other plants
Plantago lanceolata (Ribwort plantain)	Magical
Plantago major (Greater plantain)	Magical
Polypodium vulgare (Common fern)	Anecdotal oneirogenic activity

PHYTO-ONEIROGENICA: PLANTS (cont'd)

Name	Notes
Potentilla reptans (Creeping cinquefoil)	Magical, anecdotal oneirogenic activity
Randia dumetorum (Bushy gardenia)	Alternative attribution for *X. spinosa*
Rhodiola spp. (Rhodiola)	Possible oneirogen
Rhodiola rosea (Roseroot)	Traditional, possible oneirogen
Rosa spp. (Rose)	Magical, also in combination with other plants
Rosmarinus officinalis (Rosemary)	Magical, in combination with other plants
Ruscus hypoglossum (Spineless butcher's broom)	Magical, anecdotal oneirogenic activity
Salvia sp. (Xiwit)	Traditional, not yet identified
Salvia divinorum (Diviners' sage)	Traditional/modern
Salvia officinalis (Common sage)	Magical
Salvia sclarea (Clary sage)	Magical, also in combination
Santalum album (Sandalwood)	Magical, in combination with other plants
Scirpus atrovirens (Green bulrush)	Traditional
Silene capensis (African dream root)	Traditional
Solanum dulcamara (Bittersweet)	Traditional/magical
Solanum nigrum (Black nightshade)	Traditional/magical
Souroubea crassipetala (Witches' narcotic)	Traditional, possible oneirogen
Souroubea guianensis (Witches' narcotic)	Traditional, possible oneirogen
Syzygium aromaticum (Clove)	Magical, in combination
Tabernanthe iboga (Iboga)	Traditional/modern
Tanacetum annuum (Blue tansy)	Magical, in combination with other plants
Tanacetum vulgare (Tansy)	Magical
Thymus spp. (Thyme)	Magical
Turbina corymbosa (Morning glory)	Traditional
Turnera aphrodisiaca (Damiana)	Traditional/modern/magical, in combination with other plants
Ugni candollei (Ugni)	Traditional

PHYTO-ONEIROGENICA: PLANTS (cont'd)

Name	Notes
Valeriana officinalis (Valerian)	Anecdotal oneirogenic activity, in combination with *A. calamus*
Vanilla planifolia (Vanille)	Anecdotal oneirogenic activity
Verbena officinalis (Vervain)	Magical
Xeromphis spinosa (Emetic nut)	Traditional
Xeromphis uliginosa (Edile emeti nut)	Alternative attribution for *X. spinosa*

MYCO-ONEIROGENICA: MUSHROOMS

Name	Notes
Agrocybe semiorbicularis (--)	Possible oneirogen
Amanita gemmata (Gemmed amanita)	Contains *A. muscaria* active principles; some cases of death reported
Amanita muscaria (Fly agaric)	Traditional/modern
Amanita pantherina (Panther mushroom)	Contains *A. muscaria* active principles
Amanita regalis (Royal fly agaric)	Contains *A. muscaria* active principles
Amanita strobiliformis (Warted amanita)	Contains *A. muscaria* active principles
Astraeus hygrometricus (Barometer hearthstar)	Possible oneirogen
Boletus manicus (Nonda)	Traditional, possible oneirogen
Claviceps purpurea (Ergot)	Magical, in combination with other plants
Lycoperdon marginatum (Peeling mushroom)	Traditional
Lycoperdon mixtecorum (Mixtecs' puffball)	Traditional
Lycoperdon oblongiosporum (--)	Possible oneirogen
Lycoperdon perlatum (Warted puffball)	Traditional
Lycoperdon pyriforme (Pear-shaped puffball)	Traditional, anecdotal oneirogenic activity

MYCO-ONEIROGENICA: MUSHROOMS (cont'd)

Name	Notes
Psilocybe semilanceata (Liberty cap)	Modern, anecdotal oneirogenic activity
Rhizopogon sp. (--)	Possible oneirogen
Scleroderma verrucosum (Scaly earthball)	Possible oneirogen
Vascellum curtisii (--)	Possible oneirogen
Vascellum intermedium (--)	Possible oneirogen
Vascellum pratense (Meadow puffball)	Possible oneirogen

ZOO-ONEIROGENICA: ANIMALS

Name	Notes
Acanthurus sandvicensis (Surgeon fish)	Accidental
Giraffa camelopardalis (Giraffe)	Traditional, possible oneirogen
Kyphosus cinerascens (Pilot fish)	Accidental
Kyphosus fuscus (Silver drummer-fish)	Accidental
Kyphosus vaigiensis (Brass bream)	Accidental
Mugil cephalus (Flathead mullet)	Accidental
Mulloidichthys samoensis (Golden goat-fish)	Accidental
Myelobia smerintha (Bamboo worm)	Traditional
Neomyxus chaptalli (Uoua mullet)	Accidental
Upeneus arge (Goat fish)	Accidental

BROMATO-ONEIROGENICA: FOODS

Product	Notes
Anchovies	Anecdotal
Bananas	Anecdotal
Carrots	Anecdotal
Cereals	Anecdotal
Cheese	Anecdotal

BROMATO-ONEIROGENICA: FOODS (cont'd)

Product	Notes
Chocolate	Anecdotal
Crawfish	Anecdotal
Ice cream	Anecdotal
Meat	Anecdotal
Milk	Anecdotal
Mustard	Anecdotal
Onions	Anecdotal
Sardines	Anecdotal
Watercress	Anecdotal
Yogurt	Anecdotal

ONEIRO-CHYMICA: ENDOGENOUS AND SYNTHETIC COMPOUNDS

Endo-Oneirogenica: Endogenous Substances Produced in the Human Body

Name	Notes
1-Me-βC	MAOI compound
1-Me-THβC	MAOI compound
2-Me-βC	MAOI compound
5-MeO-DMT	Possible active compound in combination with an MAOI compound
Adrenochrome	Adrenaline derivative
Bufotenine	Possible active compound in combination with an MAOI compound
Deanol	Possible oneirogen
DMT	Possible active compound in combination with an MAOI compound
Endopsychosin	Possible oneirogen, not yet identified
Melatonin	Produced by the pineal gland
Pinoline	MAOI compound

ONEIRO-CHYMICA: ENDOGENOUS AND SYNTHETIC COMPOUNDS (cont'd)

Oneirosynthetica: Synthetic Drugs

Name	Notes
5-HTP	Serotonin precursor
Choline	Acetylcholine precursor
Cholinergics	Drugs increasing acetylcholine release
Dextromethorphan	Dissociative anaesthetic
Ether	Anaesthetic
Fenfluramine	Psychostimulant
Ketamine	Dissociative anaesthetic
Melatonin	Dream and waking cycle regulator
Methionine	Choline precursor
Nitrous oxide	Dissociative anaesthetic
Phencyclidine; analogues and similar compounds	Dissociative anaesthetic
Propofol	Anaesthetic
Serine	Choline precursor
Tiletamine	Dissociative anaesthetic
Tryptophan	Serotonin precursor
Vitamin B complex	Involved in the synthesis of serotonin, methionine, acetylcholine

Notes

Chapter 1

1. www.maps.org.
2. J. Ott, *The Age of Entheogens & The Angel's Dictionary* (Kennewick, Wash.: Natural Products Co. 1995), 100, 117–118.
3. www.maps.org.
4. J. Ott, "Pharmañopo-Psychonautics: Human Intranasal, Sublingual, Intrarectal, Pulmonary and Oral Pharmacology of Bufotenine," *Journal of Psychoactive Drugs* 33 (2001): 275.
5. J. Ott, Personal communication to B. Thomas (1999).

Chapter 4

1. www.bouncingbearbotanicals.com and www.psychoactiveherbs.com.
2. L. Hamilton, "An Experiment to Observe the Effects of Eating Substances Called Ereriba Leaves and Agara Bark," *Transactions of the Papua and New Guinea Scientific Society* 1 (1960): 16.
3. W. C. Taylor, personal communication to B. Thomas (2000).
4. B. Thomas, in press.
5. W. C. Taylor, personal communication to B. Thomas (2003).
6. B. Thomas, personal communication to G. Toro (2005).
7. www.dreamviews.com.
8. G. Appendino, personal communication to G. Toro (2003).
9. www.dreamviews.com.
10. A. Croce, personal communication to G. Toro (2005).

11. www.sun.ars-grin.gov.

12. www.dreamviews.com and www.sun.ars-grin.gov.

13. www.botanical.com; www.henriettesherbal.com; and www.sun.ars-grin.gov.

14. www.dreamviews.com.

15. G. Toro, *Sotto tutte le brume sopra tutti i rovi* (Torino: Nautilus, 2005), 105.

16. www.botanicalpreservationcorps.com.

17. www.dreamviews.com.

18. G. Toro, *Sotto tutte le brume sopra tutti i rovi* (Torino: Nautilus, 2005), 80–82.

Chapter 5

1. www.anglefire.com; www.botanical.com; www.iamshaman.com; www.kindredborne.org; www.spiritonline.com; and www.sun.ars-grin.gov.

2. G. Toro, *Sotto tutte le brume sopra tutti i rovi* (Torino: Nautilus, 2005), 110.

3. Ibid., 134–35.

Chapter 6

1. www.dreamviews.com.

2. www.lycaeum.org.

Chapter 7

1. A. Hoffer and H. Osmond, *The Hallucinogens* (New York and London: Academic Press, 1967), 452.

2. P. Stafford, *Enciclopedia psichedelica* (Roma: Cesco Ciapanna Editore, 1979), 331.

3. E. B. Britton, "A Pointer to a New Hallucinogen of Insect Origin," *Journal of Ethnopharmacology* 12 (3) (1984): 331.

Chapter 8

1. www.dreamviews.com.

2. Ibid.

Chapter 9

1. www.maps.org.
2. www.dreamviews.com.
3. Ibid.
4. www.erowid.org and www.lycaeum.org.
5. Ibid.
6. Ibid.
7. Ibid.
8. Ibid.
9. Ibid.
10. D. Mas De Xaxars, Personal communication to G. Toro (2006).
11. www.dreamviews.com.
12. D. Mas De Xaxars, Personal communication to G. Toro (2006).
13. www.redpoll.pharmacy.ualberta.ca.
14. D. Mas De Xaxars, Personal communication to G. Toro (2006).
15. www.botanical.com.
16. www.redpoll.pharmacy.ualberta.ca.
17. www.dreamviews.com.
18. Ibid.

Bibliography

Aldunate Del Solar, C. "Perrimontuelawen. Plantas visionarias de los Mapuches (Chile)." *Eleusis. Journal of Psychoactive Plants and Compounds* 6–7 (n.s.) (2002–2003): 103–26.

Allen, R. F., and B. Holmstedt. "The Simple β-Carboline Alkaloids." *Phytochemistry* 19 (1980): 1573–82.

Alm, T. "Ethnobotany of *Rhodiola rosea (Crassulaceae)* in Norway." *SIDA* 21 (1) (2004): 321–44.

———. "*Pinguicula vulgaris (Lentibulariaceae)* and Its Uses in Norway." *SIDA* 21 (4) (2005): 2249–74.

Antrobus, J. "Dreaming: Cortical Activation and Perceptual Thresholds." *Journal of Mind Behaviour* 7 (1986): 193–212.

———. "REM and NREM Sleep Reports: Comparison of World Frequencies by Cognitive Classes." *Psychophysiology* 5 (1983): 562–68.

Bandner, B., et al. "Dreams, Images and Emotions Associated with Propofol Anaesthesia." *Anaesthesia* 52 (8) (1997): 750–55.

Barrau, J. "Nouvelles observations au sujet des plantes hallucinogènes d'usage autochtone en Nouvelle-Guinée." *Journal d'Agriculture Tropical et de Botanique Appliqué* 5 (1958): 377–78.

———. "Observations et travaux récents sur les végétaux hallucinogènes de la Nouvelle-Guinée." *Journal d'Agriculture Tropical et de Botanique Appliqué* 9 (1962): 245–49.

Bastida, J., et al. "*Narcissus nivalis:* A New Source of Galanthamine." *Planta Medica* 56 (1990): 123–24.

Baudelaire, C. P. *Les Paradis Artificiels: Opium et Haschisch*. Paris: Poulet-Malassis et De Broise, 1860.

Beal, J. L., and E. Reinhard, eds. *Natural Products as Medicinal Agents*. Stuttgart: Hippokrates Verlag, 1981.

Beckstrom-Sternberg, S. M., and J. A. Duke. *Phytochemical Database*. Washington: United States Department of Agriculture, 1992.

Beer, A. G. "Beiträge zur Pharmakologie des extrapyramidalen Systems. I. Mitteilung: Die Wirkung des Harmins bei Katzen mit intaktem Nervensystem." *Archiv für Experimentell Pathologie und Pharmakologie* 193 (1939): 377–92.

———. "Beiträge zur Pharmakologie des extrapyramidalen Systems. II. Mitteilung: Die Wirkung des Harmins bei Katzen ohne Neocortex." *Archiv für Experimentell Pathologie und Pharmakologie* 193 (1939): 393–407.

Beningthon, J. H., and H. C. Heller. "Restoration of Brain Energy Metabolism as the Function of Sleep." *Progress in Neurobiology* 45 (1995): 347–60.

Berger, M. "Kröten, Fische, Skorpione und andere Entheogene. Die Welt der psychoaktiven Tiere." *Entheogene* 13 (2003): 277–92.

Birch, A. J., and K. M. C. Mostyn. "A New Sesquiterpene Alcohol from *Himantandra baccata* Bail." *Australian Journal of Chemistry* 8 (1954): 550–51.

Bolognini, S. (Cur.). *Il sogno cento anni dopo*. Torino: Bollati Boringhieri, 2000.

Bosinelli, M., and P. Cicogna (Cur.). *Psychology of Dreaming*. Bologna: CLUEB, 1984.

———. *Sogni: figli d'un cervello ozioso*. Torino: Bollati Boringhieri, 1991.

Bosinelli, M., et al. "The Tonic-Phasic Model and the Feeling of Self-Participation in Different Stages of Sleep." *Italian Journal of Psychology* 1 (1974): 35–65.

Bown, D. *Aroids: Plants of the Arum Family*. Portland: Timber Press, 2000.

Britton, E. B. "A Pointer to a New Hallucinogen of Insect Origin." *Journal of Ethnopharmacology* 12 (3) (1984): 331–33.

Broadley, K. J., and D. R. Kelly. "Muscarinic Receptor Agonists and Antagonists." *Molecules* 6 (2001): 142–93.

Brown, R. P., et al. "*Rhodiola rosea*: A Phytochemical Overview." *Journal of American Botanical Council* 56 (2002): 40–52.

Buresova, M., et al. "Human Circadian Rhythm in Serum Melatonin in Short Winter Days and in Simulated Artificial Long Days." *Neuroscience Letters* 136 (1992): 173–76.

Callaway, J. "A Proposed Mechanism for the Visions of Dream Sleep." *Medical Hypotheses* 26 (1988): 119–24.

Callaway, J., et al. "Endogenous β-Carbolines and Other Indole Alkaloids in Mammals." *Integration. Journal for Mind-moving Plants and Culture 5* (1994): 1–14.

Calvo, J. M., et al. "Prolonged Enhancement of REM Sleep Produced by Carbachol Microinjection into the Amygdala." *Neuroreport* 7 (2) (1996): 577–80.

Castoldi, A. *Il testo drogato. Letteratura e droga tra Ottocento e Novecento.* Torino: Einaudi, 1994.

Choochote, W., et al. "Lavicidal, Adulicidal and Repellent Effects of *Kaempferia galanga.*" *Southeast Asian Journal of Tropical Medicine and Public Health* 3 (1999): 470–76.

Collins, D. J., et al. *Plants for Medicines: A Chemical and Pharmacological Survey of Plants in the Australian Region.* Melbourne: CSIRO, 1990.

Costa, E., and M. Sandler (Eds.). *Monoamine Oxidases—New Vistas.* New York: Raven Press, 1972.

D'Albertis, L. M. *New Guinea: What I Did and What I Saw.* London: Sampson Low, Marston, Searle, and Rivington, 1880.

Díaz, J. L. "Etnofarmacología de algunos psicotrópicos vegetales de México." *Cuadernos Científicos CEMEF* 4 (1975): 135–201.

———. "Ethnopharmacology and Taxonomy of Mexican Psychodysleptic Plants." *Journal of Psychedelic Drugs* 11 (1–2) (1979): 71–101.

Drew, S., and E. Davies. "Effectiveness of *Ginkgo biloba* in Treating Tinnitus: Double-Blind, Placebo-Controlled Trial." *British Medical Journal* 322 (2001): 1–6.

Drucker-Colin, R. "Chemical Signals for Different Kinds of Sleep." *WFSRS Newsletter* 3 (1994): 8–9.

Efron, D. H., et al., eds. *Ethnopharmacologic Search for Psychoactive Drugs.* Washington: Public Health Service Publication, United States Government Printing Office, 1967.

Ernst, E., and G. Stevinson. "*Ginkgo biloba* for Tinnitus: a Review." *Clinical Otorhinolaryngology* 24 (1999): 164–67.

Fericgla, J. M., ed. *Plantas, Chamanismo y Estados de Conciencia.* Barcelona: Los Libros de la Liebre de Marzo, 1994.

Ferini-Strambi, L., et al. "Effect of Melatonin on Sleep Microstructure: Preliminary Results in Healthy Subjects." *Sleep* 16 (8) (1993): 744–47.

Festi, F., and A. Bianchi. "*Amanita muscaria.* Myco-pharmacological Outline and Personal Experiences." *Psychedelic Monographs and Essays* 5 (1991): 209–50.

Festi, F., and G. Alliotta. "Piante psicotrope spontanee o coltivate in Italia." *Annali del Museo Civico di Rovereto* 5 (1990): 135–66.

Festi, F. "Le erbe del diavolo 2. Botanica, chimica e farmacologia." *Altrove* 2 (1995): 117–45.

Font Quer, P. *Plantas medicinales.* Barcelona: Edciones Península, 1999.

Foulkes, D. "Dream Reports from Different Stages of Sleep" *Journal of Abnormal Social Psychology* 65 (1962): 14–25.

Freud, S. *L'interpretazione dei sogni.* Roma: Newton Compton, 2004.

Giacomoni, L. *Les champignons. Intoxication, pollutions, responsabilités. Un nouvelle approche de la mycologie.* Malakoff: Éd. Billes, 1989.

———. "Place des champignons et des végétaux parmi les substances psychodysleptiques et plus particulièrement parmi les hallucinogènes vrais." *Bulletin Fédération Mycologique Dauphiné-Savoie* 175 (2004): 5–31.

Gibson, C. J., and M. H. Chase (Cur.). *Sleep Disorders: Basic and Clinical Research* New York: Spectrum, 1983.

Goldstein, R., and S. Pavel. "REM Sleep Suppression in Cats by Melatonin." *Brain Research Bulletin* 7 (1981): 723–24.

Goodman, L. S., and A. Gilman, eds. *The Pharmacological Basis of Therapeutics.* New York: The MacMillan Publishing Co. Inc., 1975.

Gottlieb, A. *Legal Highs.* Manhattan Beach: Twentieth-Century Alchemist, 1973.

Goutarel, R., et al. "Pharmacodynamics and Therapeutic Actions of Iboga and Ibogaine." *Psychedelic Monographs and Essays* 6 (1993): 71–111.

Gritti, I., et al. "Projections of GABAergic and Cholinergic Basal Forebrain Neurons to the Mediodorsal Nucleus of the Thalamus." *Pflugers Archives European Journal of Physiology* 424 (1993): R46.

Guarnaccia, M. "Cibo e sogni." *Altrove* 10 (2003): 129–33.

Habán, M., et al., eds. *3rd Conference on Medicinal and Aromatic Plants of Southeast European Countries.* Nitra: Slovak University of Agriculture, 2004.

Haddon, A. C. *Reports of the Cambridge Anthropological Expedition to Torres Strait.* Cambridge: Arts and Crafts, Cambridge University Press, 1912.

Hamilton, L. "An Experiment to Observe the Effects of Eating Substances Called Ereriba Leaves and Agara Bark." *Transactions of the Papua and New Guinea Scientific Society* 1 (1960): 16–18.

Harvey, A. L. "The Pharmacology of Galanthamine and its Analogues." *Pharmacological Therapy* 68 (1995): 113–28.

Henty, E. E. "Two Drug Plants in Native Culture." *Transactions of the Papua and New Guinea Scientific Society* 1 (1960): 19–20.

Herr, B. "The Expressive Character of Fijian Dream and Nightmare Experience." *Ethnos* 9 (4) (1981): 331–52.

Hirst, M. "Root, Dream and Myth. The Use of the Oneirogenic Plant *Silene capensis* among the Xhosa of South Africa." *Eleusis. Journal of Psychoactive Plants and Compounds* 4 (n.s.) (2000): 121–49.

Hobson, J. A. *La scienza dei sogni. Alla scoprta dei segreti del sonno.* Milano: Mondadori Editore, 2003.

Hobson, J. A., and R. W. McCarley. "The Brain as a Dream Generator: An Activation Synthesis. Hypothesis of the Dream Process." *American Journal of Psychiatry* 134 (1977): 1335–48.

Hobson, J. A., et al. "Sleep Cycle Oscillation: Reciprocal Discharge by Two Brain Stem Neuronal Groups." *Science* 189 (1975): 55–58.

Hoffer, A., and H. Osmond. *The Hallucinogens.* New York and London: Academic Press, 1967.

Imeri, L., et al. "M_1 and M_3 Muscarinic Receptors: Specific Roles in Sleep Regulation." *Neuroreport* 3 (1992): 276–78.

———. "Selective Blockade of Different Brain Stem Muscarinic Receptor Subtypes: Effects on the Sleep-wake Cycle." *Brain Research* 636 (1994): 68–72.

Jansen, K. *Ketamine: Dreams and Realities.* Sarasota: MAPS, 2001.

Johnston, J. F. *The Chemistry of Common Life.* New York: D. Appleton & Co., 1857.

Jouvet, M. "The Role of Monoamines and Acetylcholine-Containing Neurons in the Regulation of the Sleep-Waking Cycle." *Ergebnisse Physiologie* 64 (1972): 166–302.

Jünger, E. *Annäherungen: Drogen und Rausch.* Stuttgart: E. Klett Verlag, 1970.

Kanjanapothi, D., et al. "Toxicity of Crude Rhizome Extract of *Kaempferia galanga* L. (Proh Hom)." *Journal of Ethnopharmacology* 90 (2004): 359–65.

Kiuchi, F., et al. "Studies on Crude Drugs Effective on Visceral Larva Migrans II. Larvicidal Principles of *Kaempferia rhizoma.*" *Chemical and Pharmaceutical Bulletin.* 36 (1988): 412–15.

Koella, W. P. (Cur.) *Sleep 1982*. Basel: Karger, 1983.

Koella, W. P., et al. (Cur.). *Sleep 1986*. Stuttgart: Fisher Verlag, 1988.

Laberge, S., and H. Rheingold. *Exploring the World of Lucid Dreaming*. New York: Random House, 1990.

Lavie, P. "Commentary to Foulkes, D.: Dreaming and REM Sleep." *WFSRS Newsletter* 3 (1994): 14.

Lemmens, R. H. M. J., and N. Bunyapraphatsara, eds. *Plant Resources of South East Asia (PROSEA)*. Leiden: Backhuys Publishers, 2003.

Lewin, L. *Phantastica*. Rochester, VT.: Park Street Press, 1998.

Mancia, M. *Il sogno come religione della mente.*Bari: Laterza, 1987.

———. *Sonno & sogno*. Bari: Laterza, 1996.

Mancia, M., et al. "Basal Forebrain and Hypothalamic Influences upon Brain Stem Neurons." *Brain Research* 107 (1976): 487–97.

———. "GABAergic Synchronizing Influences of Basalforebrain and Hypothalamic Preoptic Regions on the Mediodorsal Nucleus of the Thalamus." *Sleep Research* 22 (1993): 444.

Manske, R. H. F., and H. L. Holmes, eds. *The Alkaloids*. New York: Academic Press, 1967.

Mantegazza, P. "Sulle virtù igieniche e medicinali della coca e sugli alimenti nervosi in generale." *Annali Università di Medicina* 167 (1858): 449–519.

Mayagoitia, L., et al. "Psychopharmacologic Analysis of an Alleged Oneiro-genic Plant, *Calea zacatechichi*." *Journal of Ethnopharmacology* 18 (3) (1986): 229–43.

McGinty, D. J., et al. (Cur.). *Brain Mechanisms of Sleep*. New York: Raven Press, 1985.

Mokkhasmit, M., et al. "Study on Toxicity of Thai Medicinal Plants." *Bulletin of the Department of Medical Sciences* 12 (1971): 36–65.

Morgan, A. *Toads and Toadstools. The Natural History, Folklore, and Cultural Oddities of a Strange Association*. Berkeley: Celestial Arts, 1995.

Nakao, M., and C. Shibu. "Kaempferia galanga L." *Yakugaku Zasshi* 44 (1924): 913.

Noro, et al. "Monoamine Oxidase Inhibitor from the Rhizomes of *Kaempferia galanga* L." *Chemical and Pharmaceutical Bulletin* 31 (9183): 2708–11.

Ortega, A., et al. "Salvinorin, A New *Trans*-Neoclerodane Diterpene from *Salvia divinorum* (Labiatae)." *Journal of Chemical Society Perkins Transactions* 1 (1982): 2505–8.

Otero Aira, L. *Las plantas alucinógenas.* Barcelona: Editorial Paidotribo, 2001.

Othoman, R., et al. "Vasorelaxant Effects of Ethyl Cinnamate Isolated from *Kaempferia galanga* on Smooth Muscles of the Rat Aorta." *Planta Medica* 68(7) (2002): 655–57.

Ott, J. *Ayahuasca Analogues: Pangæan Enthogens.* Kennewick, Wash.: Natural Products Co., 1994.

———. *Pharmacotheon: Entheogenic Drugs, Their Plant Sources and History.* Kennewick: Natural Products Co., 1996.

———. "Pharmañopo-Psychonautics: Human Intranasal, Sublingual, Intra-rectal, Pulmonary and Oral Pharmacology of Bufotenine." *Journal of Psychoactive Drugs* 33 (2001): 273–81.

———. "Psychoactive Card IV: *Salvia divinorum* Epling et Játiva." *Eleusis. SISSC Information Bulletin* 4 (o.s.) (1996): 31–39.

———. *The Age of Entheogens & The Angel's Dictionary.* Kennewick: Natural Products Co., 1995.

Pancharoen, O., et al. "Cyclohexane diepoxides from *Kaempferia rotunda.*" *Phytochemistry* 43 (1996): 305–8.

Pefetti, G. G. "Allucinazioni: una prospettiva sulla psicofisiologia degli stati di coscienza." *Altrove* 11 (2004): 9–19.

Pendell, D. *Pharmako/Poeia. Plant Powers, Poisons, and Herbcraft.* San Francisco: Mercury House, 1995.

Perry, L. M., and J. Metzger. *Medicinal Plants of East and Southeast Asia. Attributed Properties and Uses.* Cambridge: The Massachusetts Institute of Technology Press, 1980.

Pletscher, A. "Über pharmakologische Beeinflußung de Zentralnervensystems durch kurzwirkende Monoaminoxidasehemmer aus der Gruppe der Harmala-Alkaloide." *Helvetica Physica et Pharmaceutica Acta* 17 (1959): 202–14.

Proskurnina, N. F., and A. P. Yakovleva. "Alkaloids of *Galanthus woronowii.*" *Journal of General Chemistry of the USSR,* 22 (1952): 1941–44.

Putnam, H. *Books, Manuscripts, and Drawings Relating to Tobacco from the Collection of George Arents, Jr. on Exhibition at the Library of Congress, April 1938.* Washington: United States Government Printer, 1938.

Rainnie, D. G., et al. "Adenosine Inhibition of Mesopontine Cholinergic Neurons: Implications for EEG Arousal." *Science* 623 (1994): 689–92.

Rätsch, C. *The Encyclopedia of Psychoactive Plants: Ethnopharmacology and Its Applications*. Rochester, Vt.: Park Street Press, 2005.

———. "*Maidal,* the Nepalese 'Sleeping Gas'." *Eleusis. Journal of Psychoactive Plants and Compounds* 6–7 (n.s.) (2002–2003): 159–66.

———. *Räucherstoffe. Der Atem des Drachen*. Aarau: AT Verlag, 1996.

———. *Schamanenpflanze. Tabak*. Solothurn: Nachtschatten Verlag, 2002.

———. *The Dictionary of Sacred and Magical Plants*. Bridport: Prism Press, 1992.

Reay, M. "The Sweet Witchcraft of Kuma Dream Experience." *Mankind* 5 (1962): 459–63.

Ruck, C. A. P., et al. "Entheogens." *Journal of Psychedelc Drugs* 11(1–2) (1979): 145–46.

Rudgley, R. *Encyclopedia of Psychoactive Substances*. New York: Thomas Dunne Books/St. Martin's Griffin, 2000.

Samorini, G. "A Contribution to the Discussion of the Ethnobotany of the Eleusinian Mysteries." *Eleusis. Journal of Psychoactive Plants and Compounds* 4 (n.s.) (2000): 3–53.

———. "A Contribution to the Ethnomycology and Ethnobotany of Alpine Psychoactive Vegetables." *Acta Phytotherapeutica* 2 (2002): 59–65.

———. (Cur.). *Amanita muscaria*. Torino: Nautilus, 1998.

———. "Funghi allucinogeni italiani." *Annali del Museo Civico di Rovereto* Suppl. Vol. 8 (1992): 125–50.

———. *Gli allucinogeni nel mito. Racconti sulle origini delle piante psicoattive*. Torino: Nautilus, 1995.

———. "Psychoactive Plants Traditionally Used in Madagascar." *Eleusis. Journal of Psychoactive Plants and Compounds* 2 (n.s.) (1999): 90–92.

———. "The Bwiti Religion and the Psychoactive Plant *Tabernanthe iboga* (Equatorial Africa)." *Integration. Journal for Mind-moving Plants and Culture* 5 (1995): 105–14.

Santaniello, E. (Cur.). *Enciclopedia della Chimica Garzanti*. Milano: Garzanti, 1998.

Schlözer, A. L. von. *Briefweschsel meist statistischen Inhalts*. Göttingen: Johann Christian Dieterich, 1775.

Schultes, R. E. "Peyote and Plants Used in the Peyote Ceremony." *Botanical Museum Leaflets,* Harvard University 4(8) (1937): 129–52.

———. "Peyote *(Lophophora williamsii)* and Plants Confused with It." *Botanical Museum Leaflets,* Harvard University 5(5) (1937): 61–88.

Schultes, R. E., and A. Hofmann. *The Botany and Chemistry of Hallucinogens.* Springfield, Ill.: C. C. Thomas, 1980.

Schultes, R. E., A. Hofmann, and C. Rätsch. *Plants of the Gods: Their Sacred, Healing, and Hallucinogenic Powers.* Rochester, Vt.: Healing Arts Press, 2001.

Schultes, R. E., and R. F. Raffauf. *Vine of the Soul.* Oracle: Synergetic Press, 1992.

Schultes, R. E., and S. Von Reis, eds. *Ethnobotany: Evolution of a Discipline.* Portland: Dioscorides Press, 1995.

Sergio, W. "Use of DMAE (2-dimethylaminoethanol) in the Induction of Lucid Dreams." *Medical Hypotheses* 26(4) (1988): 255–57.

Shulgin, A. T., and A. Shulgin. *PIHKAL: A Chemical Love Story.* Berkeley: Transform Press, 1991.

Shulgin, A. T., and H. O. Kerlinger. "Isolation of Methoxyeugenol and Trans-Isoelemicin from Oil of Nutmeg." *Die Naturwißenschaften* 51 (1964): 360–61.

Siegel, R. K. *Intoxication: The Universal Drive for Mind-Altering Substances.* Rochester, Vt.: Park Street Press, 2005.

Sitaram, N., et al. "The Effect of Physostigmine on Normal Human Sleep and Dreaming." *Archives of General Psychiatry* 35(10) (1978): 1239–43.

Skolnick, R. "β-Carbolines and Benzodiazapine Receptors: Structure-Activity Relationships and Pharmacological Activity." *Progress in Clinical and Biological Research* 90 (1982): 122.

Slotkin, T. A. "Blood Levels and Urinary Excretion of Harmine and its Metabolites in Man and Rats." *Journal of Pharmacological and Experimental Therapy* 173 (9170): 26–30.

Snow, J. "On the Inhalation of the Vapour of Ether in Surgical Operations." *British Journal of Anaesthesia* 25(1) (1953): 53–67; 25(2): 162–69; 25(3): 253–67; 25(4): 349–82.

Souccar, T. *La guía de los nuevos estimulantes.* Barcelona: Editorial Paidotribo, undated.

Stafford, P. *Enciclopedia psichedelica.* Roma: Cesco Ciapanna Editore, 1979.

Stijve, T. "The Royal Fly-Agaric, *Amanita regalis* (Fr.) Michael, A Rare Toxic and Probably Psychoactive Mushroom." *Eleusis. Journal of Psychoactive Plants and Compounds* 8 (n.s.) (2004): 55–64.

Strassman, R. *DMT: The Spirit Molecule.* Rochester: Park Street Press, 2001.

Suffia, G. "*Salvia divinorum*. Una pianta sacra poco nota." *Altrove* 8 (2001): 133–48.

Sung, T. V., et al. "Sesquiterpenoids from the roots of *Homalomena aromatica*." *Phytochemistry* 31(10) (1992): 3515–20.

The Entheogen Review, "Smoked Scorpion?" *The Entheogen Review* 10 (4) (2001): 150–51.

Thomas, B. "*Boletus manicus* Heim." *Journal of Psychoactive Drugs* 35(3) (2003): 393–94.

———. "*Galbulimima belgraveana*, 'Agara' Bark." *The Entheogen Review* 14(1) (2005): 104–5.

———. "*Kaempferia galanga*." *The Entheogen Review* 15 (1) (2006): 30–31.

———. "Psychoactive Card XI: *Galbulimima belgraveana* (F. Muell.) Sprague." *Eleusis.Journal of Psychoactive Plants and Compounds* 2 (n.s.) (1999): 82–88.

———. "Psychoactive Card XIII: *Boletus manicus* Heim." *Eleusis. Journal of Psychoactive Plants and Compounds* 4 (n.s.) (2000): 167–74.

———."Psychoactive Plant Use in Papua New Guinea." *Eleusis. Journal of Psychoactive Plants and Compounds* 4 (n.s.) (2000): 151–65.

———. "Psychoactive properties of *Galbulimima* bark." *Journal of Psychoactive Drugs* 37 (1) (2005): 109–11.

———. "The Effects Induced by the 'Agara' Bark *(Galbulimima belgraveana)*, Australia." *Eleusis: Journal of Psychoactive Plants and Compounds* 9 (2005): 91–97.

———. "The Psychoactive Flora of Papua New Guinea." *Journal of Psychoactive Drugs* 35(2) (2003): 285–93.

Thomas, J. *Prescription Products Guide, 1987*. West Melbourne: Australian Pharmaceutical Publishing Company Ltd., 1987.

Todorova, M., et al. "The Composition of *Homalomena aromatica* Schott Oil of Vietnamese Origin." *Flavour and Fragrance Journal* 3(4) (1988): 455–69.

Toro, G. *Animali psicoattivi. Stati di coscienza e sostanze di origine animale.* Torino: Nautilus, 2004.

———. "*Kyphi*: A travel into another world through a psychoactive composition of Ancient Egypt." *Magister Botanicus. Magische Blätter* 6 (2005): 13–18.

———. "Psicodelicos endogenos: triptaminas y otros compuestos." *Cañamo* 85 (2005): 100–103.

———. "Psychoactive Mushrooms: between Mycochemistry and Mycomithology." *Bulletin de l'A.E.M.B.A.* 43 (2004): 1–7.

Toro, G. *Sotto tutte le brume sopra tutti i rovi. Stregoneria e farmacologia degli unguenti.* Torino: Nautilus, 2005.

Valdés III, L. J., et al. "Divinorin A, a Psychotropic Terpenoid, and Divinorin B from the Hallucinogenic Mexican Mint *Salvia divinorum.*" *Journal of Organic Chemistry* 49 (24) (1984): 4716–20.

Valnet, J. *Fitoterapia. Guarire con le piante.* Firenze-Milano: Giunti Editore, 2005.

Voogelbreinder, S. "Psychoactive Card XV: *Lycopodiaceae Mirbel.*" Eleusis. *Journal of Psychoactive Plants and Compounds* 6–7 (n.s.) (2002–2003): 141–57.

Wade, A., ed. *The Extra Pharmacopoeia.* London: Pharmaceutical Press, 1982.

Waldhauser, F., et al. "Sleep Laboratory Investigations on Hypnotic Properties of Melatonin." *Psychopharmacology* 100 (1990): 222–26.

Weil, A. T. "Nutmeg as a Psychoactive Drug." *Journal of Psychedelic Drugs* 3 (2) (1971): 72–80.

Wilbert, J. *Tobacco and Shamanism in South America.* New Haven: Yale University Press, 1987.

Oneiropaedia Index
of Cited Species
and Compounds

Plants

Scientific names

Acacia retinoides, 35, 109

Achillea millefolium, 71, 109

Aconitum napellus, 69

Acorus calamus, 43, 58, 63, 67, 71, 109, 114

Aesculus californicus, 61, 109

Aesculus pavia, 61, 109

Allium cepa, 72, 109

Aloysia triphylla, 72, 109

Alpinia galanga, 46

Alpinia officinarum, 46

Apium graveolens, 70, 71

Areca catechu, 50, 101

Argemone mexicana, 61, 109

Argemone platyceras, 61, 109

Artemisia absinthium, 4, 58, 109

Artemisia dracunculoides, 72, 109

Artemisia vulgaris, 48, 72, 109

Arum maculatum, 35, 109

Asclepias syriaca, 35, 109

Atropa belladonna, 69, 109

Balsamodendron myrrha, 70

Banisteriopsis caapi, 29

Banisteriopsis rusbyana, 29

Bernoullia flammea, 61, 109

Borago officinalis, 58–59, 109

Boswellia sacra, 75, 109

Boswellia thurifera, 68

Brugmansia spp., 29–30, 109

Cacalia cordifolia, 43

Cacalia decomposita, 43

Calea zacatechichi, 4, 5, 11, 12, 13, 14, 15, 30–31, 64, 81, 109

Calendula officinalis, 72, 109

Cananga odorata, 75, 76, 109

Cannabis sativa, 4, 31, 59, 109

Casimiroa edulis, 30, 31–32, 109

Centella asiatica, 75, 76, 109

Cestrum spp., 35, 110

Cicuta virosa, 69

Cinnamomum camphora, 45, 72, 83, 110

Cinnamomum verum, 67

Cinnamomum zeylanicum, 72, 110

Citrus bergamia, 75, 76, 110

Citrus nobilis, 75, 76, 110

Clematis spp., 32

Clematis hirsutissima, 32

Traditional and Popular Names

Mushrooms

Scientific Names

Traditional and Popular Names

Animals

Scientific names

Traditional and Popular Names

Foods

chestnuts, 91

chocolate, 63, 93, 116

crawfish, 92, 116

garlic, 91

ice cream, 93, 116

legumes, 91

meat, 92, 103, 116

milk, 83, 93, 116

mustard, 93, 116

onions, 72, 91, 93, 116

sardines, 93, 116

watercress, 92, 116

yogurt, 93, 116

Natural and Synthetic Compounds

Δ^9-Tetrahydrocannabinol (Δ^9-THC), 4

1'-acetoxychavicol acetate, 46

1'-acetoxyeugenol acetate, 46

1-deoxy-1-thioheptaethylene glycol, 102

1-methyltetrahydro-β-carboline (1-Me-THβC), 96

1-methyl-β-carboline (1-Me-βC), 96

2,2-dimethylaminoethanol (DMAE, deanol), 98

2-MDP, 99

2-methyl-β-carboline (2-Me-βC), 96

3-[(1s)-1-(dimethylamino)ethyl] phenol, 102

3-chloro-9-ethyl-6,7,8,9,10,11-hexahydro-7,11-methanocyclooct a[b]quinolin-12-amine, 102

3-hydroxy-4-methoxyallylbenzene, 46

3-methoxy-4,5-methylenedioxyamph etamine (MMDA), 51

3,4-methylenedioxyamphetamine (MDA), 51

5-hydroxy-N,N-dimethyltryptamine (5-OHDMT,bufotenine), 87

5-hydroxytryptamine (5-HT, serotonin), 96

5-hydroxytryptophan (5-HTP), 96

5-methoxy-N,N-dimethyltryptamine (5-MeO-DMT), 85

6-hydroxytetrahydro-β-carboline (6-OH-THβC), 96

6-methoxytetrahydro-β-carboline (6-MeO-THβC, pinoline), 96

6-α-hydroxylycopodine, 49

9-N-phenylmethylaminotacrine, 102

12-epi-lycodoline, 49

acetylcholine, 25, 47, 76, 98, 100, 102, 103, 117

acetyl cinnamate, 67

acetyleugenol, 76

aconitine, 83

acorine, 58

acrifoline, 49

actinidine, 73

adrenochrome, 98, 116

aesculin, 61

alkaloid J (GB 18), 40

ambenonium, 101

amyrine, 72

anemonine, 32

anethole, 73

anhydrolycodoline, 48

annotinine, 48

arecoline, 101

atropine, 30, 40, 69

aucubin, 74

baeocystin, 78

benzaldehyde, 67

benz(f)isoquinolines, 99

benzoic acid, 62

benzomorphans, 99

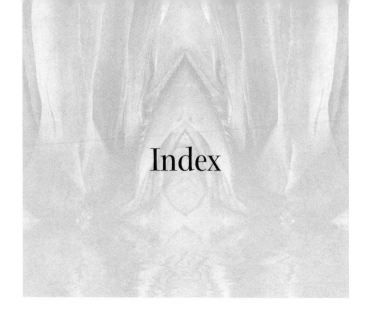

Index

Books of Related Interest

DMT: The Spirit Molecule
A Doctor's Revolutionary Research into the Biology of
Near-Death and Mystical Experiences
by Rick Strassman, M.D.

Sacred Vine of Spirits: Ayahuasca
Edited by Ralph Metzner

Sacred Mushroom of Visions: Teonanácatl
A Sourcebook on the Psilocybin Mushroom
Edited by Ralph Metzner

The Encyclopedia of Psychoactive Plants
Ethnopharmacology and Its Applications
by Christian Rätsch
Foreword by Albert Hofmann

Visionary Plant Consciousness
The Shamanic Teachings of the Plant World
Edited by J. P. Harpignies

Toltec Dreaming
Don Juan's Teachings on the Energy Body
by Ken Eagle Feather

The Dreamer's Book of the Dead
A Soul Traveler's Guide to Death, Dying, and the Other Side
by Robert Moss

The World Dream Book
Use the Wisdom of World Cultures to Uncover Your Dream Power
by Sarvananda Bluestone, Ph.D.

Inner Traditions • Bear & Company
P.O. Box 388
Rochester, VT 05767
1-800-246-8648
www.InnerTraditions.com

Or contact your local bookseller